Practice Papers for SQA Exams

Intermediate 2 | Units 1, 2 and 3

Mathematics

Text © 2009 Ken Nisbet
Design and layout © 2009 Leckie & Leckie

02/020212

ISBN 978-1-84372-778-1

Published by
Leckie & Leckie Ltd
An imprint of HarperCollins*Publishers*
Westerhill Road, Bishopbriggs, Glasgow, G64 2QT
T: 0844 576 8126   F: 0844 576 8131
leckieandleckie@harpercollins.co.uk   www.leckieandleckie.co.uk

A CIP Catalogue record for this book is available from the British Library.

Questions and answers in this book do not emanate from SQA. All of our entirely new and original Practice Papers have been written by experienced authors working directly for the publisher.

MIX
Paper from
responsible sources
FSC® C007454

FSC™ is a non-profit international organisation established to promote the responsible management of the world's forests. Products carrying the FSC label are independently certified to assure consumers that they come from forests that are managed to meet the social, economic and ecological needs of present and future generations, and other controlled sources.

Find out more about HarperCollins and the environment at
www.harpercollins.co.uk/green

Introduction

Layout of the Book

This book contains practice exam papers, which mirror the actual SQA exam as much as possible. The layout, paper colour and question level are all similar to the actual exam that you will sit, so that you are familiar with what the exam paper will look like.

The solutions section is at the back of the book. The full worked solution is given to each question so that you can see how the right answer has been arrived at. The solutions are accompanied by a commentary which includes further explanations and advice. There is also an indication of how the marks are allocated and, where relevant, what the examiners will be looking for. Reference is made at times to the relevant sections in Leckie & Leckie's book 'Intermediate 2 Maths Revision Notes'.

Revision advice is provided in this introductory section of the book, so please read on!

How to use This Book

The Practice Papers can be used in two main ways:

1. You can complete an entire practice paper as preparation for the final exam. If you would like to use the book in this way, you can either complete the practice paper under exam style conditions by setting yourself a time for each paper and answering it as well as possible without using any references or notes. Alternatively, you can answer the practice paper questions as a revision exercise, using your notes to produce a model answer. Your teacher may mark these for you.

2. You can use the Topic Index at the front of this book to find all the questions within the book that deal with a specific topic. This allows you to focus specifically on areas that you particularly want to revise or, if you are mid-way through your course, it lets you practise answering exam-style questions for just those topics that you have studied.

Revision Advice

Work out a revision timetable for each week's work in advance – remember to cover all of your subjects and to leave time for homework and breaks. For example:

Day	6pm–6.45pm	7pm–8pm	8.15pm–9pm	9.15pm–10pm
Monday	Homework	Homework	English Revision	Chemistry Revision
Tuesday	Maths Revision	Physics Revision	Homework	Free
Wednesday	Geography Revision	Modern Studies Revision	English Revision	French Revision
Thursday	Homework	Maths Revision	Chemistry Revision	Free
Friday	Geography Revision	French Revision	Free	Free
Saturday	Free	Free	Free	Free
Sunday	Modern Studies Revision	Maths Revision	Modern Studies	Homework

Make sure that you have at least one evening free a week to relax, socialise and re-charge your batteries. It also gives your brain a chance to process the information that you have been feeding it all week.

Arrange your study time into one hour or 30 minutes sessions, with a break between sessions e.g. 6pm–7pm, 7.15pm–7.45pm, 8pm–9pm. Try to start studying as early as possible in the evening when your brain is still alert and be aware that the longer you put off starting, the harder it will be to start!

Study a different subject in each session, except for the day before an exam.

Do something different during your breaks between study sessions – have a cup of tea, or listen to some music. Don't let your 15 minutes expanded into 20 or 25 minutes though!

Have your class notes and any textbooks available for your revision to hand as well as plenty of blank paper, a pen, etc. You should take note of any topic area that you are having particular difficulty with, as and when the difficulty arises. Revisit that question later having revised that topic area by attempting some further questions from the exercises in your textbook.

Revising for a Maths Exam is different from revising for some of your other subjects. Revision is only effective if you are trying to solve problems. You may like to make a list of 'Key Questions' with the dates of your various attempts (successful or not!). These should be questions that you have had real difficulty with.

Key Question	1st Attempt		2nd Attempt		3rd Attempt	
Textbook P56 Q3a	18/2/10	X	21/2/10	√	28/2/10	√
Practice Exam A Paper1 Q5	25/2/10	X	28/2/10	X	3/3/10	
2008 SQA Paper, Paper2 Q4c	27/2/10	X	2/3/10			

The method for working this list is as follows:

1. Any attempt at a question should be dated.

2. A tick or cross should be entered to mark the success or failure of each attempt.

3. A date for your next attempt at that question should be entered:

   for an unsuccessful attempt – 3 days later

   for a successful attempt – 1 week later

4. After two successful attempts remove that question from the list

   (you can assume the question has been learnt!)

Using 'The List' method for revising for your Maths Exam ensures that your revision is focused on the difficulties you have had and that you are actively trying to overcome these difficulties.

Finally forget or ignore all or some of the advice in this section if you are happy with your present way of studying. Everyone revises differently, so find a way that works for you!

Transfer Your Knowledge

As well as using your class notes and textbooks to revise, these practice papers will also be a useful revision tool as they will help you to get used to answering exam style questions. You may find as you work through the questions that you find an example that you haven't come across before. Don't worry! There may be several reasons for this. You may have come across a question on a topic that you have not yet covered in class. Check with your teacher to find out if this is the case. Or it may be the case that the wording or the context of the question is unfamiliar. This is often the case with reasoning questions in the Maths Exam. Once you have familiarised yourself with the worked solutions, in most cases you will find that the question is using mathematical techniques with which you are familiar. In either case you should revisit that question later to check that you can successfully solve it.

Trigger Words

In the practice papers and in the exam itself, a number of 'trigger words' will be used in the questions. These trigger words should help you identify a process or a technique that is expected in your solution to that part of the question. If you familiarise yourself with these trigger words, it will help you to structure your solutions more effectively.

Trigger Word	Meaning/ Explanation
Evaluate	Carry out a calculation to give an answer that is a value.
Hence	You must use the result of the previous part of the question to complete your solution. No marks will be given if you use an alternative method that does not use the previous answer.
Simplify	This means different things in different contexts: Surds: reduce the number under the root sign to the smallest possible by removing square factors. Fractions: one fraction, cancelled down, is expected. Algebraic expressions: get rid of brackets and gather all like terms together.
Give your answer to…	This is an instruction for the accuracy of your final answer. These instructions must be followed or you will lose a mark.
Algebraically	The method you use must involve algebra e.g. you must solve an equation or simplify an algebraic equation. It is usually stated to avoid trial-and-improvement methods or reading answers from your calculator.
Justify your answer	This is a request for you to indicate clearly your reasoning. Will the examiner know how your answer was obtained?
Show all your working	Marks will be allocated for the individual steps in your working. Steps missed out may lose you marks.

In the Exam

Watch your time and pace yourself carefully. Some questions you will find harder than others. Try not to get stuck on one question as you may later run out of time. Rather return to a difficult question later. Remember also that if you have spare time towards the end of your exam, use this time to check through your solutions. Often mistakes are discovered in this checking process and can be corrected.

Become familiar with the exam instructions. The practice papers in this book have the exam instructions at the front of each exam. Also remember that there is a formuae list to consult. You will find this at the front of your exam paper. However, even though these formulae are given to you, it is important that you learn them so that they are familiar to you. If you are continuing with Mathematics next session it will be assumed that these formulae are known in next year's exam!

Read the question thoroughly before you begin to answer it – make sure you know exactly what the question is asking you to do. If the question is in sections e.g. 15a, 15b, 15c, etc. then it is often the case that answers obtained in the earlier sections are used in the later sections of that question.

When you have completed your solution read it over again. Is your reasoning clear? Will the examiner understand how you arrived at your answer? If in doubt then fill in more details.

If you change your mind or think that your solution is wrong, don't score it out unless you have another solution to replace it with. Solutions that are not correct can often gain some of the marks available. Do not miss working out. Showing step-by-step working will help you gain maximum marks even if there is a mistake in the working.

Use these resources constructively by reworking questions later that you found difficult or impossible first time round. Remember: success in a Maths exam will only come from actively trying to solve lots of questions and only consulting notes when you are stuck. Reading notes alone is not a good way to revise for your Maths exam. Always be active, always solve problems.

Good luck!

TOPIC INDEX

	A Paper 1	A Paper 2	B Paper 1	B Paper 2	C Paper 1	C Paper 2	Knowledge for Prelim — Have difficulty	Knowledge for Prelim — Still needs work	Knowledge for Prelim — OK	Knowledge for SQA Exam — Have difficulty	Knowledge for SQA Exam — Still needs work	Knowledge for SQA Exam — OK
Unit 1												
Percentages & Sig. Figs.	1											
Volumes of Solids		5		2		2, 8						
Linear Relationships		5	4	10	4	8						
Algebraic Operations	2, 8	3	1	1, 6	1, 9							
Circles	6	2, 6		3		5, 10						
Unit 2												
Trigonometry	7	9		8		7, 10						
Simultaneous Equations		1	2, 3	7	3	3						
Graphs, Charts & Tables		4	2, 3		2							
Statistics	4	7		4		4						
Unit 3												
Further Algebra	5	8, 12	6	11	7	11						
Quadratic Equations/Graphs		10	7	5	8	1, 6						
Graphs												
Further Trigonometry	3	11	5	9	5, 6	9						

In the answers, there are references to the pages of Leckie & Leckie's *Intermediate 2 Maths Revision Notes* (ISBN 978-1-898890-14-0). These will help you learn more about any topics you might find difficult. You could also check out Questions in *Intermediate 2 Maths* (ISBN 978-1-84372-148-2) for graded practice of these topics.

Practice Exam A

Mathematics | Intermediate 2 | Units 1, 2 and 3

Practice Papers
For SQA Exams

Exam A
Intermediate 2
Units 1, 2 and 3
Paper 1
Non-calculator

You are allowed 45 minutes to complete this paper.

Do **not** use a calculator.

Try to answer all of the questions in the time allowed, including all of your working.

Full marks will only be awarded where your answer includes any relevant working.

Scotland's leading educational publishers

FORMULAE LIST

Cosine rule: $a^2 = b^2 + c^2 - 2bc \cos A$ or $\cos A = \dfrac{b^2 + c^2 - a^2}{2bc}$

Sine rule: $\dfrac{a}{\sin A} = \dfrac{b}{\sin B} = \dfrac{c}{\sin C}$

Area of a triangle: Area $= \frac{1}{2}ab \sin C$

Volume of a cylinder: Volume $= \pi r^2 h$

Volume of a cone: Volume $= \frac{1}{3}\pi r^2 h$

Volume of a sphere: Volume $= \frac{4}{3}\pi r^3$

Standard deviation: $s = \sqrt{\dfrac{\Sigma(x - \bar{x})^2}{n-1}} = \sqrt{\dfrac{\Sigma x^2 - (\Sigma x)^2 / n}{n-1}}$, where n is the sample size.

The roots of $ax^2 + bx + c = 0$ are $x = \dfrac{-b \pm \sqrt{(b^2 - 4ac)}}{2a}$

Marks

1. The diagram shows a toy spinner.

   The metal cone at the base of the spinner has radius
   2 centimetres and height of 6 centimetres as shown.
   Calculate the volume of the cone.
   Take π = 3·14

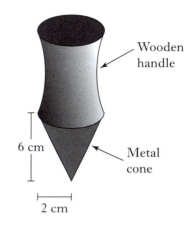

Wooden handle

6 cm

Metal cone

2 cm

2

2. Multiply out the brackets and collect like terms

   $(2x + 3y)(x - 2y)$

2

3. Part of the graph of $y = a \cos bx°$ is shown in the diagram.

   y
   2
   1
   0
   180   360   x
   −1
   −2

   State the values of a and b.

2

4. Tina and her family are playing a board game. There are two packs of cards:

   Month Cards   Bonus Cards

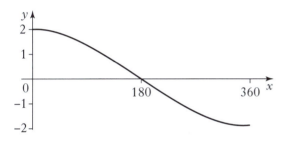

   2 3 6 10

   During her turn Tina picks a 'Month card' and a 'Bonus card'. This table shows all the possible outcomes for Tina:

	1	2	3	4
February	(F, 1)			
April	(A, 1)			
July	(J, 1)	(J, 3)		
November	(N, 1)			

   (a) Copy and complete the table

1

   (b) What is the probability that Tina picks 'November' along with a bonus that is an odd number?

2

	Marks

5. (a) Express

$$\sqrt{125} - 4\sqrt{5}$$

as a surd in its simplest form.

2

(b) Express

$$\frac{5x\,(x+3)}{x^2 + x - 6} \text{ in its simplest form.}$$

2

6.

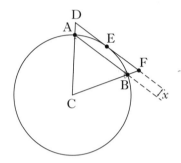

A circle, centre C, has radius of length 5 cm. Chord AB is drawn as shown and has length 6 cm.

A tangent DF is drawn to the circle with point of contact E.

Tangent DF is parallel to chord AB.

Calculate the distance, x centimetres, between the two parallel lines AB and DF.

3

7. A Biologist was studying the length of time if took bees to return to their hive. These 'out-of-hive' times are shown in this stem and leaf diagram.

Out-of-hive times (minutes)

```
0 | 5 6 7 7 8 9
1 | 2 2 5 | 8 9 9 9
2 | 3 5
3 | 4 7 8
```
$n = 18$ $2\,|\,5$ represents 25 minutes

(a) Use the above data to calculate

   (i)   The median

1

   (ii) The lower quartile

1

   (iii) The upper quartile

1

   (iv) The semi-interquartile range

1

(b) For a second hive the semi-interquartile range was found to be 3 minutes. Make a valid comparison concerning the 'out-of-hive' times for the two hives. Give a reason for your answer.

1

	Marks

8. (a) $x^2 - 2x - 15$ is expressed in the form $(x + a)(x + b)$.

Find the values of a and b if $a > b$

2

(b) Hence or otherwise write down the roots of the equation $x^2 - 2x - 15 = 0$

1

(c) The graph of $y = x^2 - 2x - 15$ is shown in the diagram.

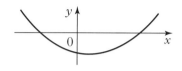

Find the coordinates of the turning point.

3

[End of Question Paper]

Mathematics | Intermediate 2 | Units 1, 2 and 3

Practice Papers
For SQA Exams

**Exam A
Intermediate 2
Units 1, 2 and 3
Paper 2**

You are allowed 1 hour, 30 minutes to complete this paper.

A calculator can be used.

Try to answer all of the questions in the time allowed, including all of your working.

Full marks will only be awarded where your answer includes any relevant working.

Scotland's leading educational publishers

FORMULAE LIST

Cosine rule: $a^2 = b^2 + c^2 - 2bc \cos A$ or $\cos A = \dfrac{b^2 + c^2 - a^2}{2bc}$

Sine rule: $\dfrac{a}{\sin A} = \dfrac{b}{\sin B} = \dfrac{c}{\sin C}$

Area of a triangle: Area $= \frac{1}{2}ab \ \sin C$

Volume of a cylinder: Volume $= \pi r^2 h$

Volume of a cone: Volume $= \frac{1}{3}\pi r^2 h$

Volume of a sphere: Volume $= \frac{4}{3}\pi r^3$

Standard deviation: $s = \sqrt{\dfrac{\Sigma(x - \bar{x})^2}{n-1}} = \sqrt{\dfrac{\Sigma x^2 - (\Sigma x)^2 / n}{n-1}}$, where n is the sample size.

The roots of $ax^2 + bx + c = 0$ are $x = \dfrac{-b \pm \sqrt{(b^2 - 4ac)}}{2a}$

Marks

1. An hotel has 22 rooms.

    The rooms are of two types: single or double.

    A single room costs £80 per night and a double room costs £120 per night

    Let x be the number of single rooms and let y be the number of double rooms

    (a) Write down an equation in x and y which satisfies the information given above. When the hotel is full the takings for that night are £2320.   1

    (b) Write down a second equation in x and y which satisfies this condition.   1

    (c) How many single rooms and how many double rooms does the hotel have?   4

2. PQ is a tangent to the circle with centre O and touches the circle at point A.

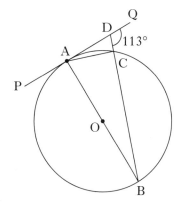

    AB is a diameter of the circle.

    Angle BDQ = 113° as shown.

    Find the size of angle BAC.   3

3. Find the equation of the line shown in the diagram which passes through the points (−2, 4) and (0, 3).   3

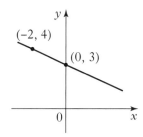

4. A vacuum cleaner production company was developing a new cleaner.

    They had four prototypes: type A, type B, type C and type D.

    A sample of households were asked to try all four cleaners for a month and then state their preference at the end of the trial.

    Their preferences are shown in this table:

Type	Frequency
A	27
B	9
C	27
D	18

    Construct a pie chart to illustrate this information. Show all your working.   3

Marks

5.

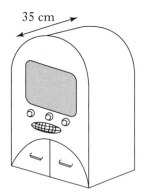

35 cm

An antique television is housed in a wooden cabinet in the shape of a prism 35 cm deep as shown in the diagram above.

The front of the cabinet is rectangular with a semicircle added at the top. The following diagram shows the measurments:

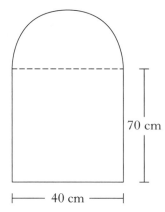

70 cm

40 cm

(*a*) Find the volume of the wooden cabinet in cubic centimetres. Give your answer correct to two significant figures.

4

At the bottom of the cabinet there are two drawers.

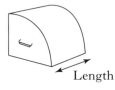

Length

The uniform cross-section of each drawer is a quarter of a circle.

The volume of each drawer is 10 000 cm³.

(*b*) Find the length of the drawer.

3

6. This clock face is showing the time four o'clock.

The minute hand, the longer of the two hands, is 8 centimetres in length.

The clock face is shown in this diagram 35 minutes later at 25 minutes to five o'clock.

Find the distance the tip of the minute hand travelled in these 35 minutes.

4

	Marks

7. A Quality Control Inspector selects a random sample of seven matchboxes produced by Machine A and records the number of matches in each box:

$$54 \quad 45 \quad 51 \quad 50 \quad 48 \quad 53 \quad 49$$

(a) For the given data calculate:

    (i)   the mean   **1**

    (ii) the standard deviation   **3**

    Show clearly all your working.

(b) Machine B was also sampled. The data gave a mean of 52 matches and a standard deviation of 1·6 matches. Compare the results for the two machines justifying your comparisons.   **2**

8. Change the subject of the formula

$$A = \frac{m^2 - n}{2} \text{ to } m$$

                                                                3

9. Mia is constructing a kite from fibre-glass rods and plastic sheeting. The frame ABCD has measurements as shown:

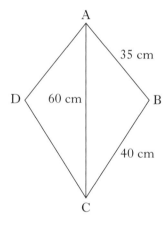

(a) Calculate the size of angle ACB.
Do not use a scale drawing.   **3**

(b) Calculate the area of plastic sheeting she needs to cover the frame.   **3**

10. Solve the equation

$$4x^2 + x - 7 = 0,$$

giving the roots correct to 1 decimal place.   **4**

11. (a) Solve the equation

    $3 \sin x° + 2 = 0, \qquad 0 \le x < 360$ **3**

(b) Prove that

$$\frac{\sin^2 x°}{1 - \sin^2 x°} = \tan^2 x°$$

                                                                 2

	Marks

12. (*a*) Express

$$x^{-\frac{1}{2}}\left(x + x^{\frac{1}{2}}\right)$$

in its simplest form.

2

(*b*) Express

$$\frac{4a^2}{b} \times \frac{3b}{4a}, \quad a \neq 0, b \neq 0$$

as a fraction in its simplest form.

2

[End of Question Paper]

$$x^{-\frac{1}{2}}\left(x + x^{\frac{1}{2}}\right)$$

Practice Exam B

Mathematics | Intermediate 2 | Units 1, 2 and 3

Practice Papers
For SQA Exams

**Exam B
Intermediate 2
Units 1, 2 and 3
Paper 1
Non-calculator**

You are allowed 45 minutes to complete this paper.

Do **not** use a calculator.

Try to answer all of the questions in the time allowed, including all of your working.

Full marks will only be awarded where your answer includes any relevant working.

Scotland's leading educational publishers

FORMULAE LIST

Cosine rule: $a^2 = b^2 + c^2 - 2bc \cos A$ or $\cos A = \dfrac{b^2 + c^2 - a^2}{2bc}$

Sine rule: $\dfrac{a}{\sin A} = \dfrac{b}{\sin B} = \dfrac{c}{\sin C}$

Area of a triangle: Area $= \frac{1}{2} ab \sin C$

Volume of a cylinder: Volume $= \pi r^2 h$

Volume of a cone: Volume $= \frac{1}{3} \pi r^2 h$

Volume of a sphere: Volume $= \frac{4}{3} \pi r^3$

Standard deviation: $s = \sqrt{\dfrac{\Sigma(x - \bar{x})^2}{n - 1}} = \sqrt{\dfrac{\Sigma x^2 - (\Sigma x)^2 / n}{n - 1}}$, where n is the sample size.

The roots of $ax^2 + bx + c = 0$ are $x = \dfrac{-b \pm \sqrt{(b^2 - 4ac)}}{2a}$

		Marks

1.

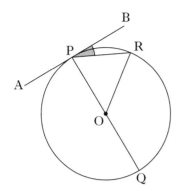

AB is a tangent to the circle, centre O, with point of contact P.

POQ is a diameter and PR is a chord.

The shaded angle BPR = 22°

Calculate the size of angle ROQ.

3

2. The shoe sizes of a group of 20 students were recorded.

6	7	8	7½	9	7½	7	8	7½	9
7½	7½	8	7	6½	8	7½	6½	8½	7½

(a) Construct a frequency table for this data and add a cumulative frequency column.

2

(b) What is the probability that one of the students picked at random has shoe size greater than 7½?

1

3. The following data gives the ages of the workers on oil rig Alpha:

21	22	24	23	27	23	23
24	21	22	23	23	21	29
23	19	23	21	24	22	23

(a) Construct a dot plot for this data.

2

(b) For this data find:

    (i) The median;

1

    (ii) The lower quartile;

1

    (iii) The upper quartile.

1

(c) For the workers on oil rig Beta the semi-interquartile range of their ages is 3·5 years. Make an appropriate comment on the distribution of the ages of the workers on the two oil rigs.

2

4.

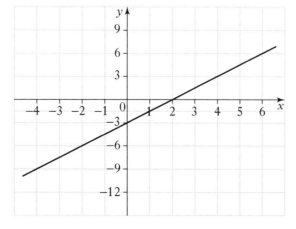

Find the equation of the line shown in the diagram.

3

Marks

5. Part of the graph of $y = k \sin ax°$ is shown in the diagram.

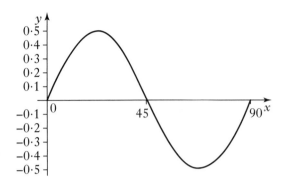

State the values of k and a.

2

6. The area of this rectangle is $10\sqrt{2}$ cm².

It has breadth $\sqrt{10}$ cm.

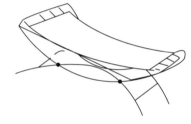

$\sqrt{10}$ cm

Calculate the length of the rectangle expressing your answer as a surd in its simplest form.

3

7. The sketch shows a hammock. Each side of the hammock consits of a metal frame in the shape of two identical parabolas.

Here is a diagram of the frame.

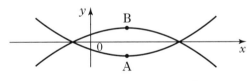

One of these parabolas has equation $y = (x - 2)^2 - 9$. The x-axis is an axis of symmetry for the two parabolas.

(a) State the coordinates of

(i) The turning point A

2

(ii) The turning point B

1

(b) Find the equation of the parabola whose equation was not given.

2

[End of Question Paper]

Mathematics | Intermediate 2 | Units 1, 2 and 3

Practice Papers
For SQA Exams

Exam B
Intermediate 2
Units 1, 2 and 3
Paper 2

You are allowed 1 hour, 30 minutes to complete this paper.

A calculator can be used.

Try to answer all of the questions in the time allowed, including all of your working.

Full marks will only be awarded where your answer includes any relevant working.

Leckie×Leckie
Scotland's leading educational publishers

FORMULAE LIST

Cosine rule: $a^2 = b^2 + c^2 - 2bc \cos A$ or $\cos A = \dfrac{b^2 + c^2 - a^2}{2bc}$

Sine rule: $\dfrac{a}{\sin A} = \dfrac{b}{\sin B} = \dfrac{c}{\sin C}$

Area of a triangle: Area $= \frac{1}{2}ab \sin C$

Volume of a cylinder: Volume $= \pi r^2 h$

Volume of a cone: Volume $= \frac{1}{3}\pi r^2 h$

Volume of a sphere: Volume $= \frac{4}{3}\pi r^3$

Standard deviation: $s = \sqrt{\dfrac{\Sigma(x - \bar{x})^2}{n - 1}} = \sqrt{\dfrac{\Sigma x^2 - (\Sigma x)^2 / n}{n - 1}}$, where n is the sample size.

The roots of $ax^2 + bx + c = 0$ are $x = \dfrac{-b \pm \sqrt{(b^2 - 4ac)}}{2a}$

| | Marks |

1. (*a*) Factorise

$2x^2 + x - 28$

$\qquad$ **2**

(*b*) Multiply out the brackets and collect like terms

$(2a - 3b)(3a + 2b) + 2ab$

$\qquad$ **3**

2. During a flu epidemic 6400 cases were recorded on Monday.

The number of cases were expected to rise by 28·5% each day.

How many cases are expected by Thursday in the same week?

Give your answer correct to three significant figures.

$\qquad$ **3**

3.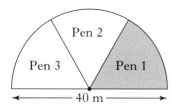

Three sheep pens are constructed from fencing. Each pen is an equal sector of a semicircle with diameter 40 metres.

Calculate the total length of fencing required to enclose pen 1, the shaded pen in the diagram.

$\qquad$ **3**

4. Temperature readings were taken each day at noon. The temperatures in °C are:

$$8 \quad 12 \quad 13 \quad 12 \quad 11 \quad 11 \quad 10$$

(*a*) Use an appropriate formula to calculate the mean and standard deviation of these temperatures.

Show clearly all your working

$\qquad$ **4**

(*b*) It was discovered that the digital thermometer used to collect the data had a malfunction and consistently recorded temperatures 2°C higher than they actually were. State the mean and standard deviation of the actual temperatures.

$\qquad$ **2**

5. Solve the equation $5x^2 - x - 3 = 0$, giving the roots correct to one decimal place.

$\qquad$ **4**

6. The diagram shows the measurements of a metal gate which is made up of 6 vertical rods and 5 horizontal rods.

(*a*) Show that the total length of rod, L cm, used to make the gate is given by $L = 11x - 2$

(*b*) Find x if the total length of rod in the gate is 713 cm.

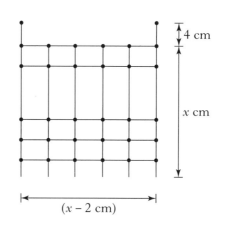

$\qquad$ **2**

$\qquad$ **1**

| | Marks |

7. Hector and Angus run a Traditional Scottish Fiddle Music Centre. On Tuesdays and Thursdays they offer tuition classes at two levels of difficulty: 'Beginners' and 'Advanced'

(a) On Tuesday 3 people turned up for the 'Beginners' class and 5 people turned up for the 'Advanced' class. The tuition fees collected that evening totalled £190. Let £x be the fee for the 'Beginners' class and let £y be the fee for the 'Advanced class'.

Write down an equation in x and y which satisfies the above condition.

1

(b) On Thursday the turn out was: 4 people for the 'Beginners' class and 2 people for the 'Advanced' class. Total takings for that evening were £132.

Write down a second equation in x and y which satisfies this condition.

1

(c) Calculate the fee for the 'Beginners' class and the fee for the 'Advanced' class.

4

8. The diagram shows a metal plate (shaded in the diagram) in the shape of a quadrilateral ABCD with measurements as shown.

Calculate:

(a) The distance between the two vertices B and D of the metal plate (the broken line in the diagram). Do not use a scale drawing.

3

(b) The area of the plate (the shaded area in the diagram).

4

Diagram: quadrilateral ABCD. Vertex A at top, with angle 79° at A. Side A to B = 4·5 cm, side A to C = 6·3 cm, side B to C = 3·6 cm, angle 15° at B below C. Vertex D at bottom right.

9. Solve the following equation for $0 \leq x \leq 360$

$3 \tan x° + 11 = 0$

3

10. The local 'Thai Cuisine' restaurant uses two types of frying pan: the traditional 'wok' in the shape of a hemisphere and a normal cylindrical pan. The measurements are shown in this diagram:

31 cm

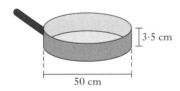
3·5 cm
50 cm

Which container has the larger capacity?

5

11. (a) Express $\dfrac{2-a}{a^2} + \dfrac{1}{a}, a \neq 0$

as a single fraction in its simplest form.

3

(b) Change the subject of the formula

$P = \sqrt{9 - Q^2}$ to Q

3

(c) Simplify $\dfrac{x^6}{4x^3 \times 2x}$

3

[End of Question Paper]

Practice Exam C

Mathematics | Intermediate 2 | Units 1, 2 and 3

Practice Papers
For SQA Exams

Exam C
Intermediate 2
Units 1, 2 and 3
Paper 1
Non-calculator

You are allowed 45 minutes to complete this paper.

Do **not** use a calculator.

Try to answer all of the questions in the time allowed, including all of your working.

Full marks will only be awarded where your answer includes any relevant working.

Leckie×Leckie

Scotland's leading educational publishers

FORMULAE LIST

Cosine rule: $a^2 = b^2 + c^2 - 2bc \cos A$ or $\cos A = \dfrac{b^2 + c^2 - a^2}{2bc}$

Sine rule: $\dfrac{a}{\sin A} = \dfrac{b}{\sin B} = \dfrac{c}{\sin C}$

Area of a triangle: Area $= \frac{1}{2} ab \sin C$

Volume of a cylinder: Volume $= \pi r^2 h$

Volume of a cone: Volume $= \frac{1}{3} \pi r^2 h$

Volume of a sphere: Volume $= \frac{4}{3} \pi r^3$

Standard deviation: $s = \sqrt{\dfrac{\Sigma(x - \bar{x})^2}{n-1}} = \sqrt{\dfrac{\Sigma x^2 - (\Sigma x)^2 / n}{n-1}}$, where n is the sample size.

The roots of $ax^2 + bx + c = 0$ are $x = \dfrac{-b \pm \sqrt{(b^2 - 4ac)}}{2a}$

	Marks

1. (*a*) Multiply out the brackets and collect like terms

$$3k + (2k - 3)(k - 4)$$

3

(*b*) Factorise

$$7\,m^2 + 54\,m - 16$$

2

2. All the passengers on a bus were asked how long they had waited before they got on the bus. The stem and leaf diagram below shows the results:

```
0 | 2  2  3  5  6  6  8  9
1 | 0  0  1  2  8
2 | 1  6
3 | 0
```

$n = 16$ $2|6$ represents 26 minutes

What is the probability that a passenger on the bus, chosen at random, waited more than 15 minutes?

1

3. This stem and leaf diagram shows the time taken, in minutes, by a group of hill walkers to complete a mountain walk.

```
 8 | 5
 9 | 3
10 | 1  2  7  9
11 | 0  3  4  7  9  9
12 | 0
```

$n = 13$ $10|7$ represents 107 minutes

(*a*) For the given data calculate:

    (i) The median

1

    (ii) The lower and upper quartiles

2

(*b*) Draw a boxplot to illustrate this data.

2

4. (*a*) State the gradient of the line shown in the diagram.

1

(*b*) Find the equation of the line.

2

(*c*) Find the coordinates of the point where the line $y = x - 1$ meets this line.

2

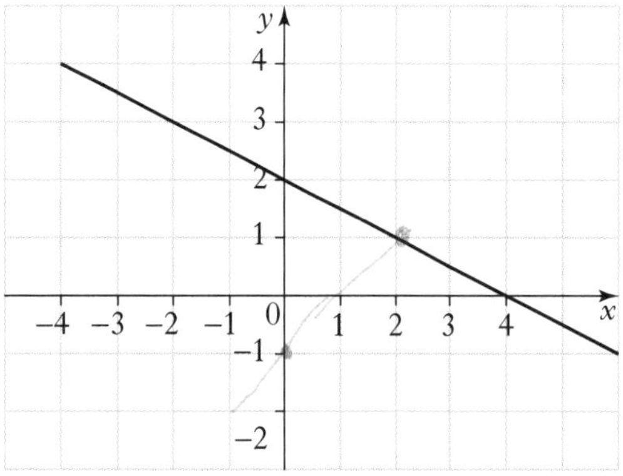

	Marks

5. Given that cos 18° = 0·951 to 3 decimal places state a value for x other than 18 for which

$\cos x° = 0·951, 0 \leq x \leq 360$ 1

6. Sketch the graph of $y = \cos 2x°, 0 \leq x \leq 360$ 3

7. Simplify

$a^{-3} \times (a^{-2})^{-2}$ 2

8. The diagram below shows the graph with equation

$y = (2x - 3)^2 + 2$

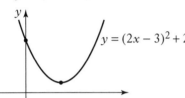

(*a*) Find the coordinates of

    (i) P, the minimum turning point   2

    (ii) Q, the intersection of the curve with the *y*-axis   1

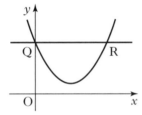

(*b*) The line through Q parallel to the *x*-axis meets the curve again at R. Find the coordinates of point R.   2

9. A drawing with dimensions

$(x + 1)$ centimetres $\times$ $(x - 2)$ centimetres

is surrounded by a frame with dimensions

$(x + 3)$ centimetres $\times$ x centimetres

The drawing and frame are shown in this diagram:

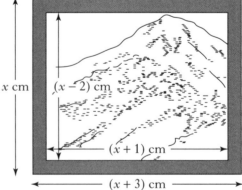

(*a*) Write down an expression, in terms of x, for the area of the drawing (with no frame)   1

(*b*) Find a simplified expression, in terms of x, for the area of the surrounding frame (shaded in the above diagram)   2

[End of Question Paper]

Mathematics | Intermediate 2 | Units 1, 2 and 3

Practice Papers
For SQA Exams

**Exam C
Intermediate 2
Units 1, 2 and 3
Paper 2**

You are allowed 1 hour, 30 minutes to complete this paper.

A calculator can be used.

Try to answer all of the questions in the time allowed, including all of your working.

Full marks will only be awarded where your answer includes any relevant working.

Leckie×Leckie
Scotland's leading educational publishers

FORMULAE LIST

Cosine rule: $a^2 = b^2 + c^2 - 2bc \cos A$ or $\cos A = \dfrac{b^2 + c^2 - a^2}{2bc}$

Sine rule: $\dfrac{a}{\sin A} = \dfrac{b}{\sin B} = \dfrac{c}{\sin C}$

Area of a triangle: Area $= \frac{1}{2} ab \sin C$

Volume of a cylinder: Volume $= \pi r^2 h$

Volume of a cone: Volume $= \frac{1}{3} \pi r^2 h$

Volume of a sphere: Volume $= \frac{4}{3} \pi r^3$

Standard deviation: $s = \sqrt{\dfrac{\Sigma(x - \bar{x})^2}{n-1}} = \sqrt{\dfrac{\Sigma x^2 - (\Sigma x)^2 / n}{n-1}}$, where n is the sample size.

The roots of $ax^2 + bx + c = 0$ are $x = \dfrac{-b \pm \sqrt{(b^2 - 4ac)}}{2a}$

	Marks

1. A graph has equation $y = x^2 - 9$

Find the coordinates of the point where it crosses the x-axis

2

2. The number of bacteria in a laboratory culture dropped by 22% per minute after being treated with an antibiotic. If there where 250000 bacteria in the culture at 10 am after treatment, how many were left by 10·03 am?

3

3. A weightlifter owns two types of circular weights:

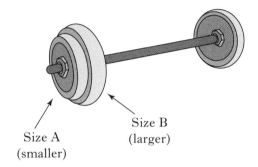

Size A
(smaller)

Size B
(larger)

Here are two arrangements of Size A and Size B weights and their corresponding total weight:

94 kg   101 kg

Find the weight of one size A weight and the weight of one size B weight.

6

4. A ream of paper contains 500 sheets.

A sample of five reams was checked and the number of sheets recorded:

$$503 \quad 504 \quad 497 \quad 495 \quad 506$$

For this data the mean number of sheets is 501.

(*a*) Calculate the standard deviation

Show clearly all your working

3

(*b*) It was felt by the producer that there was too much variation in the number of sheets in the sample.

The machine that bundled the reams was adjusted and a new sample was tested. The new mean and standard deviation for this sample were 502 sheets and 3·5 sheets respectively. Did the adjustment produce less variation?

Give a reason for your answer

1

Marks

5.

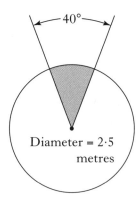

The diagram shows the plan of a Discus throwing circle for an athletics field.

The circle has diameter of 2·5 metres

For a valid throw the discus must land within the extended lines of the 40° sector of the circle.

Calculate the area of the shaded sector of the throwing circle as shown in the diagram.

3

6. Solve the equation

$$11x^2 - 2x - 1 = 0$$

giving the roots correct to two decimal places

4

7. The Ecology team at a University are dividing an area of terrain into triangular sections to study the eco-systems.

Their base camp is at Altair (A on the diagram). They use three rocks (B, C and D on the diagram) to mark out two of the triangular sections.

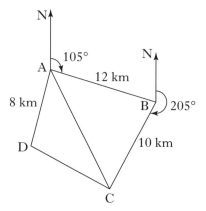

Bearings and distances are:
Rock B is 12 km from Base camp A on a bearing of 105°

Rock C is 10 km from rock B on a bearing of 205°

(*a*) Calculate the size of angle ABC

1

(*b*) Calculate the distance of rock C from the base camp at A.

3

Angle DAC is 40° with rock D being 8 km from the Base Camp at A

(*c*) Calculate the area of the triangular section ACD

2

8. The diagram on the right shows a plumb-line used by bricklayers to ensure that their constructions are vertical.

The weight at the bottom is in the shape of a cone and is made of metal.

Here are the dimensions of cone:

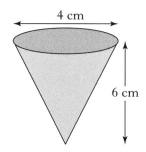

String

Conical weight

Marks

(a) Calculate the volume of this conical weight.

Give your answer correct to three significant figures.

3

(b) The weight is redesigned into the shape of half of a cylinder as shown in the diagram on the right. The same metal is used for this new weight and has the same volume as the old conical weight.

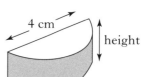

Calculate the height of this new weight.

3

9. (a) Solve the equation

$2 \tan x^\circ - 15 = 0, 0 \leq x \leq 360$

3

(b) Simplify $\dfrac{\sin x^\circ}{\tan x^\circ}$

2

10. The diagram shows a pentagon inscribed in a circle, centre O, with radius 5 cm. All sides of the pentagon are equal in length.

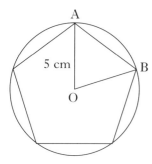

(a) Find the size of angle AOB

1

(b) Calculate the length of AB, one of the sides of the pentagon.

3

11. (a) Express $\dfrac{5}{\sqrt{3}}$ as a fraction with rational denominator

2

(b) Express $\dfrac{2}{a} - \dfrac{1}{b}$ as a single fraction in its simplest form

2

(c) Change the subject of the formula

$\dfrac{A}{p-q} = r$ to p.

3

[End of Question Paper]

Worked Answers

Substitution
- The formula $V = \frac{1}{3}\pi r^2 h$ is given to you on the formulae sheet during your exam
- The first mark is given for the correct substitution of the numbers into the formula
- You do not have access to a calculator in Paper 1 so all calculations must be done on your answer paper. This is why the value $\pi = 3\cdot14$ is given for this calculation. You must not use any other value if you are asked to use this value.

Q 1.
Volume $= \frac{1}{3}\pi r^2 h$

with $\pi = 3\cdot14$, $r = 2$ and $h = 6$

so Volume $= \frac{1}{3} \times 3\cdot14 \times 2^2 \times 6$ ✓

$\qquad = \frac{1}{3} \times 6 \times 2^2 \times 3\cdot14$

$\qquad = 2 \times 4 \times 3\cdot14$

$\qquad = 8 \times 3\cdot14$

$\qquad = 25\cdot12 \text{ cm}^3$ ✓

2 marks

Calculation
- The second mark is for correctly calculating the volume
- No marks are awarded for rounding in this question. This is generally the case in a question that does not specify the accuracy required for the answer.

See Int 2 Notes, Section 2, p. 8

Starting
- Any two correct terms among $2x^2$, $-4xy$, $3xy$ and $-6y^2$ will gain you this first mark
- The pattern used is:

remember **FOIL**

F: Firsts O: Outsides I: Insides L: Lasts

$2x \times x \quad 2x \times (-2y) \quad 3y \times x \quad 3y \times (-2y)$
$2x^2 \qquad -4xy \qquad\quad 3xy \qquad\quad -6y^2$

Q 2.
$(2x + 3y)(x - 2y)$

$\quad = 2x^2 - 4xy + 3xy - 6y^2$ ✓

$\quad = 2x^2 - xy - 6y^2$ ✓

2 marks

Completing
- Gather 'like terms': $-4xy + 3xy = -xy$

See Int 2 Notes, Section 4, p. 13

Amplitude

- a is the value of the amplitude. The given graph has a maximum value of 2 and a minimum value of −2 so the amplitude is 2 i.e. $a = 2$

Q 3.

$a = 2$ ✓

and $b = \frac{1}{2}$ ✓

2 marks

Period

- Normally (for $y = \cos x°$) there is one cycle from 0° to 360°. For the given graph there is $\frac{1}{2}$ cycle from 0° to 360°. so $b = \frac{1}{2}$. Note the period is 720° compared to 360° for $y = \cos x°$.

See Int 2 Notes, Section 12, p. 48–49

Q 4. *(a)*

	1	3	6	10
February	(F,1)	(F,3)	(F,6)	(F,10)
April	(A,1)	(A,3)	(A,6)	(A,10)
July	(J,1)	(J,3)	(J,6)	(J,10)
November	(N,1)	(N,3)	(N,6)	(N,10) ✓

1 mark

Table

- It is very important that no mistakes are made when completing the table. You will lose the mark if there is one mistake!

- Checking:

  1. Scan along each row, left to right, checking for the 1, 3, 6, 10 pattern.

  2. Scan down each column, top to bottom, checking for the F, A, J, N pattern

Probability

- Probability of an event $=$ $\dfrac{\text{Number of outcomes that make the event happen (favourable outcomes)}}{\text{Total number of outcomes}}$

- In this case there are two 'favourable outcomes: (N, 1) and (N, 3) and there are 16 possible outcomes in total – namely all the entries in the table. So you have 2 out of 16 'favourable outcomes'

Q 4. *(b)*

Probability $= \frac{2}{16} = \frac{1}{8}$ ✓

1 mark

- The mark will be awarded for $\frac{2}{16}$, cancelling down to $\frac{1}{8}$ is not essential to gain the mark

See Int 2 Notes, Section 9, p. 35–36

Q 5. *(a)*

$$\sqrt{125} - 4\sqrt{5}$$
$$= \sqrt{25 \times 5} - 4\sqrt{5}$$
$$= 5\sqrt{5} - 4\sqrt{5} \qquad ✓$$
$$= \sqrt{5} \qquad ✓$$

2 marks

Simplification
- Simplifying a surd involves removing all 'square factors'. In this case $125 = 25 \times 5$. 25 is a 'square factor'.
- You are using $\sqrt{a \times b} = \sqrt{a} \times \sqrt{b}$ for this simplification:
$$\sqrt{25 \times 5} = \sqrt{25} \times \sqrt{5} = 5 \times \sqrt{5}$$

Simplification
- Compare $5\sqrt{5} - 4\sqrt{5}$ with $5x - 4x$. You will have no difficulty simplifying $5x - 4x$ to get x. Similarly $5\sqrt{5} - 4\sqrt{5}$ gives $\sqrt{5}$

See Int 2 Notes, Section 10, p. 40

Q 5. *(b)*

$$\frac{5x(x+3)}{x^2 + x - 6}$$
$$= \frac{5x\,(x+3)}{(x-2)\,(x+3)} \qquad ✓$$
$$= \frac{5x}{x-2} \qquad ✓$$

2 marks

Factorisation
- Simplifying for example, $\frac{4}{6}$ involves knowing that $\frac{4}{6} = \frac{2 \times 2}{3 \times 2}$. There is a factor of 2 shared in the top and bottom of the fraction so 4 and 6 can both be divided by this shared factor 2. Factorising $x^2 + x - 6$ will determine if there is a shared factor

Cancelling
- $(x + 3)$ is a shared factor so both top and bottom of the fraction can be divided by $(x + 3)$ i.e. $(x + 3)$ is cancelled.

See Int 2 Notes, Section 10, p. 37

Right-angled triangle

- There are several facts that you need to gather together to solve this problem:

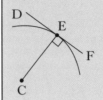

Fact 1 A tangent (DF) is perpendicular to the radius (CE) to the point of contact (E)

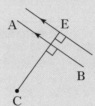

Fact 2 Any line parallel to DF will also be perpendicular to the radius CE

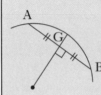

Fact 3 Any chord perpendicular to a radius is bisected by that radius. In this case G is the midpoint of chord AB.

All of these facts establish that triangle BCG is a right-angled triangle with GB = 3 cm and BC = 5 cm

Q 6.

Draw CE. This radius meets chord AB at G. CE bisects AB so AG = GB = 3cm

CE is perpendicular to chord AB so angle CGB = 90° ✓

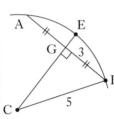

Use Pythagoras' Theorem in triangle CGB

$$CG^2 = BC^2 - BG^2$$
$$= 5^2 - 3^2 = 25 - 9 = 16$$

so $CG = \sqrt{16} = 4$ cm ✓

CE = 5 cm since CE is a radius so GE = CE − CG = 5 − 4 = 1cm

$\Rightarrow x = 1$ ✓

3 marks

Pythagoras' Theorem

- Correct use of Pythagoras' Theorem will gain you this strategy mark

- You should recognise this as a '3, 4, 5 triangle' in which case CG = 4 cm can just be written down: you will still gain this mark.

Calculation

- You have to recognise that GE is the required distance x. Notice that the radius CE is CG + GE = 4 + x so 5 = 4 + x.

See Int 2 Notes, Section 5, p. 20

Q 7. *(a) (i)*

There are 18 measurements. Divide them, in increasing order, into two groups of 9:

(5................15)(18...............38)

Median = $\frac{15+18}{2} = \frac{33}{2}$

So Median (Q_2) = 16·5 ✓

1 mark

Median

- To find the median the measurements are arranged in increasing order. The middle value is the median. If there are two middle values, as is the case in this question, then the median is the mean of the middle two values

- The mean of a and b is $\frac{a+b}{2}$

- The median is Q_2 (Q_1 and Q_3 are the lower and upper quartiles)

Q 7. *(a) (ii)*
Divide the lower 9 measurements, in increasing order, into two groups:
(5 6 7 7) 8 (9 12 12 15)
The lower quartile $(Q_1) = 8$ ✓

1 mark

Lower Quartile
- Another way of thinking about the lower quartile is that it is the median of the lower half of the measurements.
- If you read the stem-and-leaf diagram from left to right and top row down to bottom row then you are reading the measurements in increasing order

Q 7. *(a) (iii)*
Divide the upper 9 measurements, in increasing order, into two groups:
(18 19 19 19) 23 (25 34 37 38)
The upper quartile $(Q_3) = 23$ ✓

1 mark

Upper Quartile
- The upper quartile can be thought of as the median of the upper half of the measurements
- Although Q_1, Q_2 and Q_3 can be identified by counting along the numbers on the stem-and-leaf diagram it is safer to write out the measurements (9 in this case) so that no mistakes are made in counting along the measurements.

See Int 2 Notes, Section 8, p. 31

Q 7. *(a) (iv)*
Semi-interquartile range
$= \frac{1}{2} (Q_3 - Q_1)$
$= \frac{1}{2} (23 - 8) = \frac{1}{2} \times 15 = 7 \cdot 5$ ✓

1 mark

Semi-interquartile Range
- The formula $\frac{1}{2} (Q_3 - Q_1)$ is not given to you in the exam. You should memorise it!
- 'Semi' means 'half' and 'interquartile' means 'between the quartiles'. So the name 'semi-interquartile' helps you to remember the formula:

$$\frac{1}{2} (Q_3 - Q_1)$$

'Semi'   'between the quartiles'.

See Int 2 Notes, Section 8, p. 32

Q 7. *(b)*
The times for the 2nd hive are less varied in their distribution about the mean time. (semi-interquartile range is 3·5) than for the 1st hive (semi-interquartile range is 7·5 which is greater than 3·5) ✓

1 mark

Statement
- A larger semi-interquartile range means the measurements are more spread out and a smaller semi-interquartile range means the measurements are less spread out.
- It is important that you are able to communicate that you know that hive 1 times are more spread out because the semi-interquartile range, 7·5, is greater than the semi-interquartile range, 3·5, for hive 2. This comparison is crucial for gaining this mark.

See Int 2 Notes, Section 8, p. 33

Factorisation
- The correct factorisation of the quadratic expression will gain you this 1st mark.
- Remember that once you have factorised a quadratic expression you should check your answer by multiplying out:
$(x + 3)(x - 5) = x^2 - 5x + 3x - 15$
which does give $x^2 - 2x - 15$. This checking process often picks up mistakes with a negative sign.

Q 8. *(a)*
$x^2 - 2x - 15 = (x + 3)(x - 5)$
compare $(x + a)(x + b)$ ✓
$\Rightarrow a = 3$ and $b = -5$ ✓

2 marks

Values
- Notice that b is negative. Comparing each factor: $(x + 3)$ with $(x + a)$ and $(x - 5)$ with $(x + b)$ as is done in the solution will help avoid mistakes with the negative sign.

See Int 2 Notes, Section 4, p. 16

Roots
- The wording of this question may make it appear more difficult than it is.

Normally solving $x^2 - 2x - 15 = 0$
gives the working: $(x + 3)(x - 5) = 0$
$\Rightarrow x = -3$ or $x = 5$

These are precisely the negative values of a and b.
- Remember 'roots' and 'solutions' are the same. These are different words for the same thing!

See Int 2 Notes, Section 4, p. 45

Q 8. *(b)*
The roots are:
$x = -3$ and $x = 5$ ✓

1 mark

x-value
- The turning point is midway between the two x-axis intercepts
- The calculation is the mean of the two roots

Q 8. *(c)*

$x = \frac{-3+5}{2} = \frac{2}{2} = 1$ ✓

then align to get
when $x = 1$
$y = 1^2 - 2 \times 1 - 15$
$= -16$ ✓
The turning point is $(1, -16)$ ✓

3 marks

Substitution
- To find the y-coordinate of the turning point you must substitute the x-coordinate ($x = 1$) back into the formula of the parabola

Coordinates
- Coordinates are asked for so the notation for a point i.e. $(1, -16)$ must be given

WORKED ANSWERS: EXAM A   **PAPER 2**

Q 1. *(a)*
$$x + y = 22 \qquad ✓$$

1 mark

1st equation
- There is information in the question that is not needed for this equation: £80 and £120.
- The total number of rooms is 22 made up of x singles and y doubles

Q 1. *(b)*
$$80x + 120y = 2320 \qquad ✓$$

1 mark

2nd equation
- This is the 'cost equation': x rooms at £80 and y rooms at £120 giving a total income of £2320

See Int 2 Notes, Section 7, p. 25

Strategy
- An attempt to use simultaneous equations will gain you this strategy mark

Q 1. *(c)*
$$80x + 120y = 2320 \; (\div 40)$$
$$\Rightarrow 2x + 3y = 58$$
Solve:
$$\left. \begin{array}{l} x + y = 22 \\ 2x + 3y = 58 \end{array} \right\} \begin{array}{l} \times 2 \rightarrow 2x + 2y = 44 \\ \rightarrow \underline{2x + 3y = 58} \quad ✓ \end{array}$$
$$\text{Subtract:} \quad -y = -14$$
$$\Rightarrow y = 14 \qquad ✓$$
Now substitute $y = 14$ in $x + y = $
$$22 \Rightarrow x + 14 = 22 \Rightarrow x = 8 \quad ✓$$
So there are 8 single rooms
and 14 double rooms   ✓

4 marks

Values
- If you follow the correct method in your working, even making calculation errors, you can still gain this mark
- Notice that dividing by 40 greatly simplifies the 2nd equation making all the subsequent working much easier

Correct values
- Producing the correct values of x and y with the relevant working will gain you this mark.

Statement
- You have to go beyond the values of x and y by making a statement concerning the number of each type of room that the hotel has.

See Int 2 Notes, Section 7, p. 26–27

Q 2.

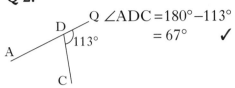

$\angle ADC = 180° - 113°$
$= 67°$ ✓

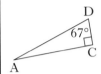

$\angle ACD = 90°$ since $\angle ACB$ is an angle in semicircle

so $\angle DAC = 90° - 67° = 23°$ ✓

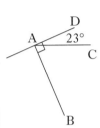

$\angle BAD = 90°$ Since PQ is perpendicular to the radius OA to the point of contact A

so $\angle BAC = 90° - 23° = 67°$ ✓

3 marks

Angle ADC
- 'straight angles' add to 180°. In this case ADQ is a 'straight angle' so $\angle ADC + \angle QDC = 180°$

Angle DAC
- AB is a diameter with C on the circumference so $\angle ACB$ is an 'angle in a semicircle'. All such angles are 90°

- DCB is a straight line so $\angle DCA + \angle ACB = 180°$

Angle BAC
- The tangent (PQ) is perpendicular to a radius (OA) to the point of contact (A) so $\angle DAB = 90°$ giving $\angle DAC + \angle CAB = 90°$

See Int 2 Notes, Section 5, p. 19–20

Q3

P(−2, 4)

Q(0, 3)

$M_{PQ} = \frac{3-4}{0-(-2)} = \frac{-1}{2}$

So gradient $= -\frac{1}{2}$ ✓

The y-intercept is (0, 3)

So the equation of the line is:

$y = -\frac{1}{2}x + 3$ (×2) ✓

$\Rightarrow 2y = -x + 6$ ✓

$\Rightarrow 2y + x = 6$

3 marks

Gradient
- The formula used here is:

$$\text{gradient} = \frac{\text{distance up or down } (y\text{-difference})}{\text{distance along } (x\text{-difference})}$$

- For the points $A(x_1, y_1)$ and $B(x_2, y_2)$

gradient of AB $(m_{AB}) = \frac{y_2 - y_1}{x_2 - x_1}$ ← y-difference
← x-difference

y-intercept
- The y-intercept (0,3) gives $c = 3$ in the formula: $y = mx + c$

Equation
- Equation of a straight line:

$$y = mx + c$$
gradient   y-intercept
(0,c)

- In this case $m = \frac{1}{2}$ and $c = 3$

- $y = -\frac{1}{2}x + 3$ will gain you this 3rd mark.

Removing the fraction and rearranging to $2y + x = 6$ is not essential, but this is a good form for questions where simultaneous equations are then required.

See Int 2 Notes, Section 3, p. 9–11

Q 4.

	Fre-quency	Frac-tion	Angle	
A:	27	$^{27}/_{81} = ^3/_9 = ^1/_3$	$^1/_3$ of $360° = 120°$	✓
B:	9	$^9/_{81} = ^1/_9$	$^1/_9$ of $360° = 40°$	
C:	27	$^{27}/_{81} = ^3/_9 = ^1/_3$	$^1/_3$ of $360° = 120°$	
D:	18	$^{18}/_{81} = ^2/_9$	$^2/_9$ of $360° = 80°$	✓

Total = 81   Total = 360°

Pie chart showing 'cleaner preference'

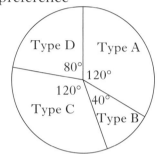

Type D 80°
Type A 120°
120° 40°
Type C Type B

✓

3 marks

Fractions of 360°
- The fraction $\frac{\text{frequency}}{\text{total}}$ gives the size of each sector of the pie chart. You find this fraction of 360° to give you the sector angle
- This mark is for knowing the method for calculation of the sector angles

Angles
- Calculation of the correct sector angles will gain you this mark
- Always check that your sector angles (in this case 120°, 40°, 120°, 80°) add up to 360°!

Pie chart
- All sectors should be labelled eg 'Type A' etc
- You should be very accurate drawing your Pie Chart as you are only allowed up to a 2° error in each angle

See Int 2 Notes, Section 8, p. 29

Q5. (a)

Semicircle

Rectangle

radius of semicircle
$= \frac{1}{2} \times 40 = 20$ cm
total area
$=$ area of $+$ area of
rectangle   semicircle
$=$ length $\times$ breadth
$\quad + \frac{1}{2} \pi r^2$ ✓
$= 70 \times 40 + \frac{1}{2} \times \pi$
$\quad \times 20 \times 20$
$= 2800 + 628·31...$
$= 3428·31...$ cm^2 ✓

Volume $=$ Area of end $\times$ depth ✓
$\quad = 3428·31 \times 35$
$\quad = 119991·14...$ ✓
$\quad \div 120000$ cm^3 ✓
(to 2 significant figures)

4 marks

Substitution
- Correct substitution of length = 70, breadth = 40 and radius = 20 into the formulae will gain you this mark
- A common error is using the diameter value (40 cm) when you should be using the radius value (20 cm). The area of a circle formula $A = \pi r^2$ uses the radius value.
- Radius $= \frac{1}{2} \times$ Diameter

Strategy
- Knowing to find the area of the end of this prism and multiply by the depth will gain you the strategy mark

Calculation
- Never round answers until the end of a long calculation like this

Rounding
- A mark is allocated for correctly rounding your answer to 2 significant figures.
- This mark can be gained even if your answer is wrong before the rounding. The mark is for knowing how to round to 2 sig figs.

Strategy
- Knowing how to find the volume of the drawer will gain you this mark

Q 5. *(b)*

$$\frac{\text{Volume of}}{\text{drawer}} = \frac{\text{Area of}}{\text{quarter circle}} \times \text{length} \checkmark$$

$$\Rightarrow 10000 = \tfrac{1}{4}\,\pi\,r^2 \times \text{length} \qquad \checkmark$$

$$\Rightarrow 10000 = \tfrac{1}{4}\,\pi \times 20^2 \times \text{length}$$

$$\Rightarrow 10000 = 314 \cdot 15\ldots \times \text{length}$$

$$\Rightarrow \frac{10000}{314 \cdot 15\ldots} = \text{length}$$

so length $= 31 \cdot 83\ldots$

$\qquad\qquad \doteq 31 \cdot 8$ cm $\qquad \checkmark$

(to 1 decimal place)

3 marks

Equation
- This time you know the volume so there is an equation to solve. You will gain this mark for correctly setting up the equation

Solving
- It is easier to calculate $\tfrac{1}{4}\,\pi \times 20^2$ first and then dividing through by the answer $314 \cdot 15\ldots$

  The alternative gives $\frac{4 \times 10000}{\pi \times 20^2}$ which is more liable to have errors creep into the calculation

- Rounding is not important here as it is not mentioned in the question - so any correct answer will do.

  See Int 2 Notes, Section 2, p. 8

Strategy
- Knowing how to find the circumference will gain you this mark
- Either $C = \pi D$ or $C = 2\pi r$ $(r = 8)$

Q 6.

Circumference of Inside

Circle $= \pi \times D$ $\qquad \checkmark$

where $D = 2 \times 8 = 16$ cm

So Circumference $= \pi \times 16 = 16\pi$ cm

Fraction of

Circumference $= \frac{35}{60} = \frac{7}{12}$ $\qquad \checkmark$

Distance travelled $= \frac{7}{12} \times 16\pi$ $\quad \checkmark$

$\qquad\qquad = 29 \cdot 32\ldots \doteq 29 \cdot 3$ cm

$\qquad\qquad$ (to 3 sig figs) $\qquad \checkmark$

4 marks

Fraction
- A complete turn i.e whole circumference is travelled in 60 minutes. Tip has travelled for 35 minutes out of 60 minutes i.e. $\frac{35}{60}$

Strategy
- To gain this mark requires evidence that you knew to find $\frac{7}{12}$ of the circumference

Calculation
- On calculator:

  $\boxed{7}\;\boxed{\div}\;\boxed{1}\boxed{2}\;\boxed{\times}\;\boxed{1}\boxed{6}\;\boxed{\times}\;\boxed{\pi}\;\boxed{\text{EXE}}$

- Any correct rounding is acceptable here

  See Int 2 Notes, Section 5, p. 17–18

Q 7. *(a) (i)*

$$\text{Mean} = \frac{54+45+51+50+48+53+49}{7}$$

$$= \frac{350}{7} = 50 \qquad \checkmark$$

1 mark

Mean
- Mean $= \dfrac{\text{sum of the numbers}}{\text{number of numbers}} = \dfrac{\Sigma x}{n} = \overline{x}$

Q 7. *(a)* *(ii)*

x	$x - \bar{x}$	$(x - \bar{x})^2$
54	4	16
45	−5	25
51	1	1
50	0	0
48	−2	4
53	3	9
49	−1	1

$$\Sigma(x - \bar{x})^2 = 56$$

✓

$$s = \sqrt{\frac{\Sigma(x - \bar{x})^2}{h-1}} = \sqrt{\frac{56}{6}} \doteq 3 \cdot 1 \text{ (to 1 dec. pl.)} ✓$$

✓

3 marks

Squared deviations
- This mark is gained for the correct last column in the table: the squared values of the deviations from the mean

Substitution
- The formula $s = \sqrt{\frac{\Sigma(x-\bar{x})^2}{h-1}}$ is given to you in the exam on your formulae page
- This mark is for correctly substituting $\Sigma(x - \bar{x})^2 = 56$ and $n - 1 = 6$ into the formula

Calculation
- If you know how to use the STAT mode on your calculator to check $5 = 3 \cdot 1$ then you should do this. Remember just writing the answer down from the calculator with no working will not gain you the marks

Q 7. *(b)*
On average there are more matches in Machine B's boxes (mean = 52 is greater than mean = 50 for machine A)
There is much more variation in the number of matches in Machine A's boxes than those from Machine B
(s = 3·1 for Machine A is greater than s = 1·6 for Machine B) ✓

✓

2 marks

1st statement
- This concerns the 'average' contents. Back up your statement with the statistics (52 and 50)

2nd statement
- This concerns the distribution about the mean. A larger standard deviation means more variation about the mean.

See Int 2 Notes, Section 9, p. 33–34

Q8.

$$A = \frac{m^2 - n}{2}$$

$(\times 2) \quad (\times 2)$

$$\Rightarrow 2A = m^2 - n \quad \checkmark$$

$(+n) \quad (+n)$

$$\Rightarrow 2A + n = m^2 \quad \checkmark$$

So $m^2 = 2A + n$

$$\Rightarrow m = \sqrt{2A + n} \quad \checkmark$$

3 marks

1st step
- Get rid of the fraction: multiply both sides of the equation by 2

2nd step
- Try to isolate the expression involving the subject m: add n to both sides

Last step
- The 'inverse' of squaring is 'square rooting' so take the square root of both sides.
- Technically you should include $-\sqrt{2A + n}$ and write $\pm\sqrt{2A + n}$ but this will not be expected (at Higher level it would!)

See Int 2 Notes, Section 10, p. 39

Q 9. *(a)*

Use the Cosine Rule
in triangle ABC $\quad \checkmark$

$$\text{Cos C} = \frac{a^2 + b^2 - c^2}{2ab}$$

$$\Rightarrow \text{Cos C} = \frac{40^2 + 60^2 - 35^2}{2 \times 40 \times 60} \quad \checkmark$$

$$= 0 \cdot 828\ldots$$

So angle $C = \cos^{-1}(0 \cdot 828\ldots)$

$$= 34 \cdot 09\ldots$$

$$\doteqdot 34 \cdot 1° \quad \checkmark$$

3 marks

Strategy
- Knowing to use the Cosine Rule will gain you this mark

Substitution
- The formula given to you in the exam on the formulae page is:
$$\cos A = \frac{b^2 + c^2 - a^2}{2bc}.$$
You should practise changing this formula to the forms: $\cos B = \frac{a^2 + c^2 - b^2}{2ac}$ and $\cos C = \frac{a^2 + b^2 - c^2}{2ac}$
- When you know the 3 sides of a triangle and are asked to find an angle then you should know to use the Cosine Rule.

Calculation
- Your calculator must be set in DEG mode. There should be a 'D' or 'DEG' on your display otherwise using $\boxed{\cos^{-1}}$ will give you the wrong answer.

See Int 2 Notes, Section 6, p. 24

Q 9.(b)
Area of triangle ABC
$= \frac{1}{2}\, ab\, \sin C$ ✓
$= \frac{1}{2} \times 40 \times 60 \times \sin 34 \cdot 09...°$ ✓
$= 672 \cdot 65 ...$ cm^2
So Area of Kite $= 2 \times 672 \cdot 65...$
$= 1345 \cdot 30...$
$\doteqdot 1350$ cm^2 ✓
(to 3 significant figures)

3 marks

Strategy
- If you know two sides and the angle in between then you use $\frac{1}{2}\, ab \sin C$ to find the area.

Substitution
- You will gain this mark for the correct substitution of $a = 40$, $b = 60$, $c = 34 \cdot 09...$ into the formula

Calculation
- Doubling gives the final area as the whole kite consists of two congruent (identical) triangles.
- Use $34 \cdot 09...$ not $34 \cdot 1$ in the calculation

See Int 2 Notes, Section 6, p. 22

Strategy
- This mark is for showing evidence in your working of an attempt to use the 'quadratic formula'
- The 'quadratic formula' is given to you in your exam on the formulae page

Q10
$4x^2 + x - 7 = 0$
compare $ax^2 + bx + c = 0$
then $a = 4$, $b = 1$ and $c = -7$
$x = \frac{-b \pm \sqrt{b^2 - 4ac}}{2a}$ ✓
$= \frac{-1 \pm \sqrt{1^2 - 4 \times 4 \times (-7)}}{2 \times 4}$ ✓
$= \frac{-1 \pm \sqrt{1 + 112}}{8}$
So $x = \frac{-1 + \sqrt{113}}{8}$ or $x = \frac{-1 - \sqrt{113}}{8}$ ✓
$x = 1 \cdot 203...$ or $x = -1 \cdot 453...$
$x \doteqdot 1 \cdot 2$ or $x \doteqdot -1 \cdot 5$ ✓
(correct to 1 decimal place)

4 marks

Substitution
- It is good practice to state the values of a, b and c
- Take care with negatives – if there is a negative in the equation it will appear as a negative value to be substituted into the formula
- Notice the use of '×' signs and that -7 is placed in brackets
- '±' means that in the final calculation you will have two different calculations: one with '+' and one with '–'

b^2-4ac
- This mark is for correctly calculating 113 under the square root sign i.e. the discriminant
- Notice that $-4 \times 4 \times (-7)$ gives a positive answer because of the two negatives.

Roots
- You must round correctly to gain the final mark since the question asks for this.
- Correct answer with no working: 0 out of 4!

See Int 2 Notes, Section 11, p. 45–46

Rearrangement
- The 1st step is to find the value of $\sin x°$

1st value
- Sin $x°$ is negative: use

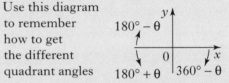

  to determine the quadrants (3rd and 4th)

- 1st quadrant angle is obtained from $\sin^{-1}(\frac{2}{3})$. Do not use the negative with $\boxed{\sin^{-1}}$

- 3rd quadrant angle is always $180° + (1^{st}$ quad angle$)$

Q 11. *(a)*

$3\sin x° + 2 = 0$

$\Rightarrow 3\sin x° = -2 \Rightarrow \sin x° = -\frac{2}{3}$ ✓

$x°$ is in the 3rd or 4th quadrants

the 1st quadrants angle is $41·8°$

So $x = 180 + 41·8$

$\quad = 221·8$

$\qquad$ or

$\quad x = 360 - 41·8$ ✓

$\quad = 318·2$ ✓

3 marks

2nd value
- 4th quadrant angle is always $360° - (1^{st}$ quad angle$)$

- Use this diagram to remember how to get the different quadrant angles

  $180° - \theta$

  $180° + \theta \quad 360° - \theta$

  (θ is the 1st quadrant angle)

See Int 2 Notes, Section 12, p. 50

Strategy
- The idea is to change $\frac{\sin^2 x°}{1-\sin^2 x°}$ by steps into $\tan^2 x°$ using known results.

- Since $\sin^2 x° + \cos^2 x° = 1$, rearrangement gives: $\cos^2 x° = 1 - \sin^2 x°$. This result allows you to replace $1 - \sin^2 x°$ by $\cos^2 x°$.

Q 11. *(b)*

Prove $\frac{\sin^2 x°}{1-\sin^2 x°} = \tan^2 x°$

Left hand side $= \frac{\sin^2 x°}{1-\sin^2 x°}$

$= \frac{\sin^2 x°}{\cos^2 x°} = \left(\frac{\sin x°}{\cos x°}\right)^2 = \tan^2 x°$ ✓

$= $ Right hand side ✓

hence the result is true

2 marks

Strategy
- You should know the result $\frac{\sin x°}{\cos x°} = \tan x°$

  This means $\frac{\sin x°}{\cos x°} \times \frac{\sin x°}{\cos x°} = \tan x° \times \tan x°$. This allows you to take the 2nd step in the proof.

See Int 2 Notes, Section 12, p. 51

Brackets

- You are using the normal 'multiplying out the brackets': $a(b + c) = ab + ac$

- The Law of Indices you are using is:

$x^m \times x^n = x^{m+n}$

- You should be aware that x can be written x^1

Q 12. *(a)*

$x^{-\frac{1}{2}} \left(x + x^{\frac{1}{2}}\right)$

$= x^{-\frac{1}{2}} \times x^1 + x^{-\frac{1}{2}} \times x^{\frac{1}{2}}$

$= x^{-\frac{1}{2}+1} + x^{-\frac{1}{2}+\frac{1}{2}}$

$= x^{\frac{1}{2}} + x^{\circ}$ ✓

$= \sqrt{x} + 1$ ✓

2 marks

Simplify

- The Laws of Indices used here are:

$a^{\circ} = 1$ and $a^{m/n} = \left(\sqrt[n]{a}\right)^m$

- You would still gain this 2nd mark if you leave $x^{\frac{1}{2}}$, however you should be aware that $x^{\frac{1}{2}} = \sqrt{x}$. Remember this:

$x^{m/n}$ ← power
← root

So $x^{\frac{1}{2}}$ ← power 1
← square root

i.e $\left(\sqrt[2]{x}\right)^1$

This is, of course, written $\sqrt{x}$!

See Int 2 Notes, Section 10, p. 41–42

Multiplication

- The rule is: $\frac{c}{d} \times \frac{e}{f} = \frac{ce}{df}$

Q 12. *(b)* $\frac{4a^2}{b} \times \frac{3b}{4a}$

$= \frac{4a^2 \times 3b}{b \times 4a} = \frac{{}^1\cancel{4} \times a \times {}^1\cancel{a} \times 3 \times \cancel{b}^1}{{}_1\cancel{b} \times \cancel{4}_1 \times \cancel{a}_1}$ ✓

$= \frac{1 \times a \times 1 \times 3 \times 1}{1 \times 1 \times 1} = \frac{3a}{1}$

$= 3a$ ✓

2 marks

Simplification

- Factors appearing on the top and bottom of the fraction can be cancelled. For instance: divide top and bottom of the fraction by a, likewise divide top and bottom by b and then by 4

- Be careful not to do this 'cancelling' process in a situation where '+' or '−' appears eg $\frac{x+2}{x}$, you cannot cancel in this case.

See Int 2 Notes, Section 10, p. 37

Q 1.

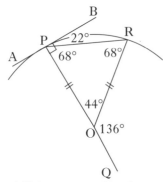

Tangent AB is perpendicular to the radius OP
So ∠OPR = 90°−22° = 68° ✓
Triangle OPR is isosceles (OP and OR are equal radii)
So ∠PRO = ∠OPR = 68°
In triangle OPR:
∠POR = 180°− (68° + 68°) = 44° ✓
⇒ ∠QOR = 180° − 44° = 136° ✓

3 marks

Tangent/Radius
- A tangent to a circle is perpendicular to the radius to the point of contact. In this case ∠OPB = 90°

Isosceles Triangle
- Any two radii in a circle are equal in length
- The angles opposite the equal sides in an isosceles triangle are themselves equal. In this case ∠OPR and ∠ORP
- The three angles in triangle OPR add up to 180°
  So ∠OPR + ∠ORP + ∠POR = 180°
  giving 68° + 68° + ∠POR = 180°
  So ∠POR = 180° − 68° − 68° = 44°

Straight Angle
- POQ is a straight line (a diameter) so ∠POR + ∠ROQ = 180°
  ⇒ 44° + ∠ROQ = 180°
  giving ∠ROQ = 180° − 44° = 136°
- You do not need to give all the reasons in your solution to gain the marks.

See Int 2 Notes, Section 5, p. 19

Q 2. *(a)*

Size	tally	frequency	cumulative frequency
6	|	1	1
6½	||	2	3
7	|||	3	6
7½	⊔⊓||	7	13
8	||||	4	17
8½	|	1	18
9	||	2	20

Total = 20 ✓✓

2 marks

frequency
- The 1ˢᵗ mark is for a correct frequency column
- It is useful to check your frequency column with a total. This should equal the number of numbers.

Cumulative frequency
- The 2ⁿᵈ mark is for the correct cumulative frequency column
- Add the next frequency number to the previous cumulative frequency number to complete this column
- Your final value (20) should equal the frequency total, if not, you have made a calculation error.

See Int 2 Notes, Section 8, p. 30

Probability

- Probability = $\dfrac{\text{Number of favourable outcomes}}{\text{Total number of outcomes}}$

In this case since there are 13 sizes that are equal to or less than $7\frac{1}{2}$ then this leaves 7 of the 20 sizes greater than $7\frac{1}{2}$. So there are 7 out of 20 giving $\frac{7}{20}$

- The crucial number 13 next to size $7\frac{1}{2}$ appears in the cumulative frequency column.

See Int 2 Notes, Section 9, p. 35–36

Q 2. *(b)*
$$\text{probability} = \frac{7}{20} \quad \checkmark$$

1 mark

Dotplot
- You should first determine the least (19) and greatest (29) of the ages as this will allow you to plan the scale.

- You have access to squared paper during your exam and you should use it for a question of this type

- Work systematically through the data placing a new dot on your dotplot for each new piece of data.

Q 3. *(a)*
Dotplot of Ages for oil rig Alpha

$\checkmark$
$\checkmark$

19 20 21 22 23 24 25 26 27 28 29
age (years)

2 marks

Completion
- Count the number of dots when you have completed your dotplot. In this case there should be 21, the same number as the pieces of data.

- Remember to give your dotplot a title and also to label the axis to give a meaning to the numbers

See Int 2 Notes, Section 8, p. 30

Q 3. *(b)* (i)
$$\text{Median} = 23 \quad \checkmark$$
$$(Q_2)$$

1 mark

Median
- The symbol Q_2 is used for the median

- For 21 ages: ($1^{st}\dots 10^{th}$) (11th) ($12^{th}\dots 21^{st}$). So when placed in increasing order the 11th age gives the median age for this data i.e 23

Q 3. *(b)* (ii)
$$\text{Lower Quartile} = \frac{21+22}{2} = 21\cdot 5 \quad \checkmark$$
$$(Q_1)$$

1 mark

Lower Quartile
- The symbol Q_1 is used for the lower quartile

- This is the median of the lower half of the ages i.e. the median of the 1st ten of the ages in increasing order: ($1^{st}\dots 5^{th}$) ($6^{th}\dots 10^{th}$). It is the mean of the 5th and 6th ages i.e. the mean of 21 and 22

Q 3. *(b)* (iii)

Upper Quartile $= \frac{23+24}{2} = 23 \cdot 5$ ✓

$\quad$ (Q_3)

1 mark

Upper Quartile
- The Symbol Q_3 is used for the upper quartile

- This is the median of the upper half of the ages i.e. the median of the 2nd group of 10 ages in increasing order: (12th... 16th) (17th... 21st). It is the mean of the 16th and 17th ages i.e. the mean of 23 and 24

See Int 2 Notes, Section 8, p. 31

Q 3. *(c)*

For oilrig Alpha:
semi-interquartile range
$= \frac{1}{2} 0 \,(23 \cdot 5 - 21 \cdot 5) = 1$ ✓
The age distribution is more spread out (about the mean age) on oilrig Beta compared to that on oilrig Alpha since the semi-interquartile range of 3·5 for Beta is greater than the 1 for Alpha. ✓

2 marks

Semi-interquartile range
- You need to calculate the statistic:
Semi-interquartile range $= \frac{1}{2}\,(Q_3 - Q_1)$ for oil rig Alpha and then compare it to the same statistic for oil rig Beta

Comparison
- It is important you back any comparison statement with the relevant statistics. In this case the semi-interquartile range: the greater the range the more spread out the data is around the mean

See Int 2 Notes, Section 9, p. 32–33

gradient
- You must take great care over the scales on each axis. On the x-axis
1 square = 1 unit but on the y axis
1 square = 3 units. It appears the gradient should be $\frac{1}{2}$ using the definition:

$$\text{gradient} = \frac{\text{distance up (or down)}}{\text{distance along}}$$

however in this case the distance up is 3 units not 1 unit. The gradient is $\frac{3}{2}$

Q 4

$\quad$ gradient $= \frac{3}{2}$ ✓
y-intercept is $(0, -3)$ ✓

equation is $y = \frac{3}{2}x - 3$ ✓
$(\Rightarrow 2y = 3x - 6 \Rightarrow 2y - 3x = -6)$

3 marks

y-intercept
- The y-intercept is where the line crosses the y-axis and this determines the value of c in "$y = mx + c$"

- Careful with the y-axis scale. The y-intercept is 1 square down which is 3 units down so $c = -3$

Equation
- You use the equation:

$$y = mx + c$$
$$\nearrow \qquad \nwarrow$$
gradient $\quad$ $(0, c)$ is the y-interept

with $m = \frac{3}{2}$ and $c = -3$

- "$y = \frac{3}{2}x - 3$" will gain you this 3rd mark. The further rearrangement given in the solution is not essential.

See Int 2 Notes, Section 3, p. 9–11

Amplitude
- In $y = k \sin ax$, k is the value of the amplitude. This is determined from the maximum and minimum value of the graph: max. value is $0 \cdot 5$, min value is $-0 \cdot 5$ so the amplitude has value $0 \cdot 5$. The amplitude is always positive.

Q 5.

$k = 0 \cdot 5$ ✓

$a = 4$ ✓

2 marks

The period
- In $y = k \sin ax$ the value of a gives the number of cycles from $0°$ to $360°$. In this case there is one cycle from $0°$ to $90°$ so there will be 4 cycles from $0°$ to $360°$

- The period is actually $90°$ which is $\left(\frac{360}{4}\right)°$. In general $y = k \sin ax$ has period $\left(\frac{360}{a}\right)°$.

See Int 2 Notes, Section 12, p. 48–49

Equation
- This 1st mark is awarded for correct substitution of Area $= 10\sqrt{2}$ and breadth $= \sqrt{10}$ into the Area formula

Q 6.

Area = length × breadth

$\Rightarrow 10\sqrt{2} = \text{length} \times \sqrt{10}$ ✓

$\Rightarrow \frac{10\sqrt{2}}{\sqrt{10}} = \text{length}$

$\Rightarrow \text{length} = \frac{10\sqrt{2} \times \sqrt{10}}{\sqrt{10} \times \sqrt{10}} = \frac{10\sqrt{20}}{10}$ ✓

$= \sqrt{20} = \sqrt{4 \times 5} = 2\sqrt{5}$ cm ✓

3 marks

Solution
- Solving the equation and 'rationalising the denominator' gains you the 2nd mark.

- Divide both sides of the equation by $\sqrt{10}$.

- 'rationalising the denominator' means getting rid of the square root sign on the bottom of the fraction. Remember in general $\sqrt{a} \times \sqrt{a} = a$.

Simplification
- Remove any 'square factors', in this case 4, from under the square root sign: $\sqrt{4} = 2$

See Int 2 Notes, Section 10, p. 40–41

x-coordinate
- The least value of $(x - 2)^2 - 9$ is $0^2 - 9$ and this occurs when $x = 2$. Remember something squared must be zero or positive, never a negative value.

Q 7. (a)(i) ✓

$A = (2, -9)$ ✓

2 marks

y-coordinate
- when $x = 2$, $y = (2 - 2)^2 - 9 = 0^2 - 9 = -9$

See Int 2 Notes, Section 11, p. 44

Q 7. *(a)* (ii)

$$B = (2,9) \qquad ✓$$

1 mark

Turning point
- By symmetry point B is the reflection of point A in the x-axis so the x-coordinate will be the same (2) and the y-coordinate positive 9.

Q 7. *(b)* The other parabola is a reflection of $y = (x - 2)^2 - 9$ in the x-axis and so has equation: ✓

$$y = -\left[(x-2)^2 - 9 \right]$$
$$\Rightarrow y = -(x-2)^2 + 9$$
$$\Rightarrow y = 9 - (x-2)^2 \qquad ✓$$

2 marks

Reflection in x-axis
- If graph $y =$ (expression is x) is reflected in the x-axis then the equation of the image or new graph is given by $y = -$(expression is x). In this case you require the negative of $(x-2)^2 - 9$

Equation
- It is better if you simplify $-\left[(x-2)^2 - 9 \right]$. In a simpler example $-(a - b) = -a + b$. Following this pattern gives $-(x-2)^2 + 9$

- Notice that, for example, $-2 + 3 = 3 - 2$ so $-(x - 2)^2 + 9$ can be written $9 - (x - 2)^2$. This is the more usual form for this expression

See Int 2 Notes, Section 11, p. 43

WORKED ANSWERS: EXAM B   **PAPER 2**

1st factor
- One correct factor will gain you this 1st mark

2nd factor
- when you have completed your factorisation you should check your answer by multiplying out using 'FOIL'
- Most mistakes are to do with the positive and negative signs. Check these carefully

See Int 2 Notes, Section 4, p. 16

Q 1. *(a)*

$2x^2 + x - 28$ ✓

$= (2x - 7)(x + 4)$ ✓

2 marks

Starting removing the brackets
- 2 correct terms will gain you this mark.
- The pattern used for multiplying out the brackets is: Firsts, Outsides, Insides, Lasts:

$$(2a - 3b)(3a + 2b)$$

Firsts	Outsides	Insides	Lasts
$2a \times 3a$	$2a \times 2b$	$-3b \times 3a$	$-3b \times 2b$
$6a^2$	$4ab$	$-9ab$	$-6b^2$

Q 1. *(b)*

$(2a - 3b)(3a + 2b) + 2ab$ ✓

$= 6a^2 + 4ab - 9ab - 6b^2 + 2ab$ ✓

$= 6a^2 - 3ab - 6b^2$ ✓

3 marks

Completing removing the brackets
- There are 4 terms with the Outsides (4ab) and Insides (−9ab) being 'like terms'

Like terms
- In this case there are 3 'like terms' namely 4ab, −9ab and 2ab which combine to give −3ab

See Int 2 Notes, Section 4, p. 12–14

Q 2.

A rise of 28·5% means there will be 128·5% the next day

Multiplication factor = 1·285 ✓

Cases on Thursday

$$= 6400 \times 1 \cdot 285^3 \quad ✓$$
$$= 13579 \cdot 6...$$
$$\doteqdot 13600 \quad ✓$$

(to 3 significant figures)

3 marks

Multiplication factor
- Starting with 6400 cases you consider this as 100% of the cases. Increasing by 28·5% will therefore give you 128·5% or $\frac{128 \cdot 5}{100} = 1 \cdot 285$.
- Each increase of 28·5% is given by a multiplication by 1·285. So three consecutive increases will be given by three such multiplications

Strategy
- × 1·285 × 1·285 × 1·285 is the same as × 1·285³
- Here is a useful diagram:

Monday (6400) Tuesday Wednesday Thursday
   × 1·285   × 1·285   × 1·285

Calculation
- Rounding correctly is important as it is mentioned in the question, so follow the instructions!

See Int 2 Notes, Section 1, p. 5

Q 3.

Six sectors would fit to make a complete circle

Arc length ✓

$$\text{Arc} = \frac{1}{6} \times \pi D \quad ✓$$
$$= \frac{1}{6} \times \pi \times 40$$
$$= 20 \cdot 94....$$

Total length of fencing
$$= 20 + 20 + 20 \cdot 94....$$
$$= 60 \cdot 94....$$
$$\doteqdot 60 \cdot 9 \text{ m (to 1 dec pl.)} \quad ✓$$

3 marks

Circumference
- Your first step is to find the circumference of the whole circle using $C = \pi D$
- None of the circle formulae are given to you on your formulae page so you must learn them!

Arc length
- This mark is awarded for knowing how to find the arc length, it is $\frac{1}{6}$ of the circumference.

Perimeter
- The two radii are part of the fencing of Pen 1 and so must be added to the arc length
- Since accuracy is not mentioned in the question any correct rounding for the answer will do.

See Int 2 Notes, Section 4, p. 17–18

Mean

- The symbol $\bar{x}$ ("x bar") is used for the mean

- Mean $= \dfrac{\text{sum of the numbers}}{\text{number of numbers}} = \dfrac{\Sigma x}{n}$

Squared Deviations

- This mark is for correctly calculating the squared deviations from the mean $(x - \bar{x})^2$. i.e. getting the last column of the table correct.

Substitution

- Correct substitution of $\Sigma(x - \bar{x})^2 = 16$ and $n - 1 = 6$ into the formula will gain this mark

Calculation

- Don't forget to take the square root and to round your answer

- The alternative formula is

$$s = \sqrt{\frac{\Sigma x^2 - (\Sigma x)^2/n}{n-1}}$$

In this case $\Sigma x^2 = 863$, $(\Sigma x)^2 = 5929$, $n = 7$ and $n - 1 = 6$ giving :

$$s = \sqrt{\frac{863 - 5929/7}{6}} = \sqrt{\frac{16}{6}} \doteq 1{\cdot}6 \text{ as before}$$

- Both formulae are given on your formulae page during the exam. The formula used in the solution opposite is usually easier to use with less possibility of making mistakes. However you should use the formula you are most comfortable using.

See Int 2 Notes, Section 9, p. 33–34

Q 4. *(a)*

Mean $= \dfrac{8+12+13+12+11+11+10}{7} = \dfrac{77}{7}$ ✓

$= 11°C$

x	$x - \bar{x}$	$(x - \bar{x})^2$
8	−3	9
12	1	1
13	2	4
12	1	1
11	0	0
11	0	0
10	−1	1

$$\Sigma(x - \bar{x})^2 = 16$$ ✓

$$s = \sqrt{\frac{\Sigma(x - \bar{x})^2}{n-1}} = \sqrt{\frac{16}{6}} = \sqrt{2.66} \ldots$$ ✓

$$= 1{\cdot}63\ldots \doteq 1{\cdot}6 \text{ °C}$$ ✓

(to 1 dec pl.)

4 marks

Mean

- All 7 numbers are reduced by 2. The total reduces by 14. Dividing by 7, therefore reduces the mean by 2

Standard Deviation

- The distribution about the mean will be unaltered so the standard deviation will remain the same

Q 4. *(b)*

New mean $= 9°C$ ✓

New standard deviation $= 1{\cdot}6°C$ ✓

2 marks

Strategy
- There are two indications in this question that you are expected to use the quadratic formula:

1st: 'correct to 1 decimal place'

2nd: 4 marks are allocated

A factorisation method does not need approximate answers and there would be fewer marks allocated.

Q 5.
$$5x^2 - x - 3 = 0$$
compare $ax^2 + bx + c = 0$
$$\Rightarrow a = 5, b = -1 \text{ and } c = -3$$
$$x = \frac{-b \pm \sqrt{b^2 - 4ac}}{2a} \quad ✓$$
$$= \frac{1 \pm \sqrt{(-1)^2 - 4 \times 5 \times (-3)}}{2 \times 5} \quad ✓$$
$$= \frac{1 \pm \sqrt{1 + 60}}{10} \quad ✓$$
So $x = \frac{1 + \sqrt{61}}{10}$ or $x = \frac{1 - \sqrt{61}}{10}$
$$\Rightarrow x = 0 \cdot 881\ldots \text{ or } x = -0 \cdot 681\ldots$$
$$\Rightarrow x \doteqdot 0 \cdot 9 \text{ or } x = -0 \cdot 7 \quad ✓$$
(both correct to 1 decimal place)

4 marks

Substitution
- Careful with negatives. Two of the replacements are negative: $b = -1$ and $c = -3$

$b^2 - 4ac$
- Note: $(-1)^2 = -1 \times (-1) = 1$. This is positive
- $-4 \times 5 \times (-3)$: again this is positive as there are two negative signs
- If your calculation of $b^2 - 4ac$ produces a negative answer in a question like this you have made a calculation error. You should check your working again.

Roots
- Careful with your calculator. Note that: $\boxed{1} \boxed{+} \boxed{\sqrt{}} \boxed{6} \boxed{1} \boxed{\div} \boxed{1} \boxed{0} \boxed{\text{EXE}}$ gives $1 \cdot 78$, the wrong answer! Either use brackets: $(1 + \sqrt{61}) \div 10$ or calculate the answer to $(1 + \sqrt{61})$ first and then divide by 10.

See Int 2 Notes, Section 11, p. 45–46

Q 6. (a)
Long vertical rods
$$= (x + 4) \text{ cm} \quad (\times 2)$$
Short vertical rods $= x$ cm $\quad (\times 4)$
Horizontal rods $= (x - 2)$ cm $\quad (\times 5)$
Total length $\quad ✓$
$$= 2(x + 4) + 4x + 5(x - 2)$$
$$= 2x + 8 + 4x + 5x - 10$$
$$= 11x - 2 \text{ cm} \quad ✓$$
so $L = 11x - 2$

2 marks

Strategy
- Identify the three different lengths of rod and the number of each type:

2 rods of length $(x + 4)$ cm: $2(x + 4)$ cm

4 rods of length x cm: $4x$ cm

and 5 rods of length $(x - 2)$ cm: $5(x - 2)$ cm

Simplification
- Since $11x - 2$ is given in the question it is very important that you show all your working clearly.

See Int 2 Notes, Section 4, p. 12–13

Q 6. *(b)*

$$L = 11x - 2 = 713$$
$$\Rightarrow 11x = 715$$
$$\Rightarrow x = \frac{715}{11} = 65 \quad \checkmark$$

1 mark

Value of x
- You should set up an equation based on the information you are given. The total length of rod is 713 cm but previously you have determined that an expression for this total is $11x - 2$. You now 'equate' these: $11x - 2 = 713$

Q 7. *(a)*

$$3x + 5y = 190 \quad \checkmark$$

1 mark

1st equation
- Interpretation is a particular difficulty in these 'simultaneous equation' questions. There is a lot of writing to interpret and to extract the necessary information from. To help you, remember there will always be two quantities that are not known. In this case the two different fees. Concentrate on one of these, say £x, the fee for the beginners class. What information is given? "3 people turned up" So 3 fees of £x giving £$3x$. Similarly for the advanced class: "5 people turned up", so 5 fees of £y giving £$5y$. In total the fees are £$(3x + 5y)$. But you are told the total fees were £190 so $3x + 5y = 190$.

Q 7. *(b)*

$$4x + 2y = 132 \quad \checkmark$$

1 mark

2nd equation
- Be careful not to mix up the xs and ys! This is a common mistake leading to the wrong equation: $2x + 4y = 132$. Your only consolation is that in part(c) you can still achieve full marks using the wrong equation

See Int 2 Notes, Section 7, p. 25

Strategy
- This mark is gained for evidence that you know this is a 'simultaneous equation' question. You will gain this mark for just 'starting' the process.

Values
- Working through to a pair of values – even if they are wrong will gain you this mark.

Correct values
- The alternative method is to find x first:

$$\left.\begin{array}{l} 3x+5y=190 \\ 4x+2y=132 \end{array}\right\} \begin{array}{l} \times 2 \to 6x+10y=380-(1) \\ \times 5 \to 20x+10y=660-(2) \end{array}$$

subtract (1) from (2): $14x = 280$

$$\Rightarrow x = \frac{280}{14} = 20$$

Then substitute in one of the two equations

- Always check, in this case use $x = 20$, $y = 26$ in $4x + 2y$ to give $4 \times 20 + 2 \times 26 = 80 + 52 = 132$

Statement
- Fees were asked for so your final statement must answer the question.

See Int 2 Notes, Section 7, p. 26–27

Q 7. *(c)*

Solve:

$$\left.\begin{array}{l} 3x+5y=190 \\ 4x+2y=132 \end{array}\right\} \begin{array}{l} \times 4 \to 12x+20y=760 \\ \times 3 \to \underline{12x+6y=396} \end{array}$$

$$\text{Subtract:} \qquad 14y = 364$$

$$\Rightarrow y = \frac{364}{14} = 26 \quad \checkmark$$

Substitute $y = 26$ in $3x + 5y = 190$

$$\Rightarrow 3x + 5 \times 26 = 190$$

$$\Rightarrow 3x + 130 = 190 \qquad \checkmark$$

$$\Rightarrow 3x = 190 - 130 = 60$$

$$\Rightarrow x = \frac{60}{3} = 20 \qquad \checkmark$$

So the 'beginner's class' costs £20 and the 'advanced class' costs £26. $\qquad \checkmark$

4 marks

Strategy
- You gain this mark if there is evidence in your solution that you knew to use the Cosine Rule.

- How do you know to use the Cosine Rule and not the Sine Rule? In this case you know side AB and side AD and the angle inbetween (the 'included' angle) angle BAD.

To use the Cosine Rule you will always need to know two sides and the included angle (if you are finding the 3rd side)

Q 8(*a*)
Use the Cosine Rule in triangle ABC: ✓
$a^2 = b^2 + d^2 - 2bd \cos A$
$= 6 \cdot 3^2 + 4 \cdot 5^2 - 2 \times 6 \cdot 3 \times 4 \cdot 5 \cos 79°$
$= 49 \cdot 12....$ ✓
So $a = \sqrt{49 \cdot 12....}$
$\quad = 7 \cdot 008....$
$\quad \doteqdot 7 \cdot 01$ cm ✓
The distance between vertex B and vertex D is approximately 7·01cm
(Correct to 3 significant figures)

3 marks

Substitution
- Your formulae page gives:

$$a^2 = b^2 + c^2 - 2bc \cos A$$

You have to know how to adapt this for a triangle named ABD:

$$a^2 = b^2 + d^2 \times 2bd \cos A$$

where $b = 6 \cdot 3$, $d = 4 \cdot 5$ and angle $A = 79°$

Calculation
- Remember to find the square root as the last step in the calculation

- You should estimate from the diagram roughly the length you would expect for the answer. If your calculated answer is not near this estimate then check your calculation.

From the diagram BD looks to be slightly longer than AD = 6·3 cm so around 7 cm is a reasonable length.

See Int 2 Notes, Section 6, p. 24

Q 8. (b)

Required Area = Area of triangle ABD − Area of triangle BCD ✓

Area of triangle BCD

$$= \tfrac{1}{2} \times BC \times BD \times \sin \hat{CBD}$$

$$= \tfrac{1}{2} \times 3 \cdot 6 \times 7 \cdot 008\ldots \times \sin 15°$$

$$= 3 \cdot 265\ldots \text{ cm}^2 \quad ✓$$

Area of triangle ABD

$$= \tfrac{1}{2} \times AB \times AD \times \sin \hat{BAD}$$

$$= \tfrac{1}{2} \times 4 \cdot 5 \times 6 \cdot 3\ldots \times \sin 79°$$

$$= 13 \cdot 914\ldots \text{ cm}^2 \quad ✓$$

Area of plate

$$= 13 \cdot 914\ldots - 3 \cdot 265\ldots$$

$$= 10 \cdot 649\ldots$$

$$\doteq 10 \cdot 6 \text{ cm}^2 \quad ✓$$

(correct to 3 significant figures)

4 marks

Strategy
- A subtraction of two areas is the plan.

1st substitution
- You use the area formula:
  Area $= \tfrac{1}{2}\, ab \sin C$ which is given on your formulae sheet.
- Do not use the rounded version from part (a) for the length of BD.

2nd substitution
- Using $\tfrac{1}{2} bd \sin A$ with $b = 6 \cdot 3$, $d = 4 \cdot 5$ and angle $A = 79°$

Calculation
- Again do not round answers before the end of the calculation as you will then be introducing errors

See Int 2 Notes, Section 6, p. 22

Q 9.

$$3 \tan x° + 11 = 0$$

$$\Rightarrow 3 \tan x° = -11$$

$$\Rightarrow \tan x° = -\frac{11}{3} \quad ✓$$

$x°$ is in the 2nd or 4th quadrants
The 1st quadrant angle is $74 \cdot 7°$
So
$$x = 180 - 74 \cdot 7 \text{ or } x = 360 - 74 \cdot 7 \quad ✓$$
$$\Rightarrow x \doteq 105 \cdot 3 \text{ or } x \doteq 285 \cdot 3 \quad ✓$$
(both correct to 1 decimal place)

3 marks

Solve for tan x
- Your first step is to rearrange to get a value for $\tan x°$.
- Substract 11 from both sides of the equation then divide both sides by 3

1st value
- You should know which quadrants $x°$ is in to give $\tan x°$ a negative value. Use:

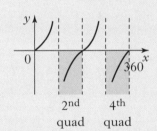

or

- The 2nd quadrant value is calculated from:
  $$180° - (1\text{st quad angle})$$

2nd value
- The 4th quadrant value is calculated from:
  $$360° - (1\text{st quad angle})$$
- Reminder: the 1st quadrant angle is obtained from $\tan^{-1}\left(\tfrac{11}{3}\right)$. Never use $\boxed{\tan^{-1}}$ with a negative value.

See Int 2 Notes, Section 12, p. 50

Q 10.

Find the two volumes ✓

The 'wok'

Volume of a sphere $= \frac{4}{3} \pi r^3$

So Volume of a hemisphere

$$= \frac{1}{2} \times \frac{4}{3} \pi r^3 = \frac{2}{3} \pi r^3$$

In this case $r = \frac{31}{2} = 15 \cdot 5$ cm ✓

So Volume $= \frac{2}{3} \times \pi \times 15 \cdot 5^3$

$\qquad = 7799 \cdot 26 .... \doteqdot 7800$ cm^3

$\qquad\qquad$ (to 3 sig figs)

The 'pan'

Volume of a cylinder $= \pi r^2 h$

In this case $r = 25$cm and

$h = 3 \cdot 5$cm

So Volume $= \pi \times 25^2 \times 3 \cdot 5$ ✓

$\qquad = 6872 \cdot 23 .... \doteqdot 6900$ cm^3

$\qquad\qquad$ (to 3 sig figs) ✓

So the 'wok' has the larger

capacity by approximately

900 cm^3 ✓

5 marks

Strategy
- Capacity' means volume. You will have to calculate the volume of each type of pan and compare these volumes.

1ˢᵗ substitution
- The formula $V = \frac{4}{3} \pi r^3$ is given to you on the formulae page during your exam

- In this case you have only half a sphere so use $\frac{1}{2}$ of $\frac{4}{3} \pi r^3$ i.e $\frac{2}{3} \pi r^3$ with r being half of the diameter of 31cm i.e. 15·5 cm.

2ⁿᵈ substitution
- The formula $V = \pi r^2 h$ is given on your formulae sheet

- In this case substitute $r = 25$ and $h = 3 \cdot 5$

Volumes
- Both volumes correct and you gain this mark

Statement
- You must clearly justify your conclusion using the values for the volume. Finding the difference and stating shows clearly that you understand the results you calculated.

See Int 2 Notes, Section 2, p. 7–8

Common Denominator
- To add, for example, $\frac{1}{2}+\frac{1}{3}$ you need to change the fractions to $\frac{3}{6}+\frac{2}{6}$ so that they have a 'common denominator' of 6.

  In this case $\frac{2-a}{a^2}+\frac{1}{a}$ cannot be added until their denominators are the same. 'a²' is the simplest such 'common denominator'.

Q 11. *(a)*

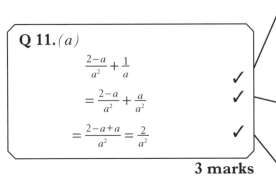

$$\frac{2-a}{a^2}+\frac{1}{a} \qquad ✓$$

$$=\frac{2-a}{a^2}+\frac{a}{a^2} \qquad ✓$$

$$=\frac{2-a+a}{a^2}=\frac{2}{a^2} \qquad ✓$$

3 marks

Equivalent fraction
- $\frac{1}{a}=\frac{1\times a}{a\times a}=\frac{a}{a^2}$. You are always allowed to multiply (or divide) the top and bottom of a fraction by the same number or expression

Simplify
- $\frac{3}{6}+\frac{2}{6}=\frac{3+2}{6}$: the numerators are added once the denominators are the same. In this case the numerators are $2-a$ and a giving $2-a+a=2$

  See Int 2 Notes, Section 10, p. 38–39

1ˢᵗ step
- Your aim is to isolate the letter Q. 1ˢᵗ step is to remove the square root. This is done by squaring both sides

Q 11. *(b)*

$$P=\sqrt{9-Q^2}$$
$$\Rightarrow P^2=9-Q^2 \qquad ✓$$
$$\Rightarrow Q^2=9-P^2 \qquad ✓$$
$$\Rightarrow Q=\sqrt{9-P^2} \qquad ✓$$

3 marks

2ⁿᵈ step
- Add Q^2 to both sides and substract P^2 from both sides. This isolates Q^2.

Final step
- To remove the 'squaring' you must 'square root' both sides

- Technically you should write $\pm\sqrt{9-P^2}$ but will not be penalised for not doing this!

  See Int 2 Notes, Section 10, p. 39

Simplify Powers
- The denominator is simplified first:

  $4x^3\times 2x^2=4\times x\times x\times x\times 2\times x\times x$
  $=8x^5$

- Or use the Index Law: $a^m\times a^n=a^{m+n}$

Q 11. *(c)*

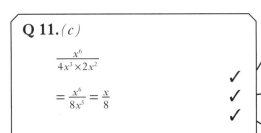

$$\frac{x^6}{4x^3\times 2x^2}$$

$$=\frac{x^6}{8x^5}=\frac{x}{8} \qquad \begin{array}{c}✓\\✓\\✓\end{array}$$

3 marks

Simplify fraction
- Use the Index Law: $\frac{a^m}{a^n}=a^{m-n}$. In this case you have $\frac{x^6}{x^5}=x^{6-5}=x^1=x$

Coefficients
- Obtaining the 8 from the coefficients 4 and 2 will gain you a mark.

  See Int 2 Notes, Section 10, p. 41–42

Start brackets

- You should use this pattern:

$$\underbrace{(2\overbrace{k - 3) \; (k}^{\text{Firsts} \quad \text{Lasts}} - 4)}_{\text{Insides}}$$

Outsides

to give (FOIL):

$$2k \times k \quad 2k \times (-4) \quad -3 \times k \quad -3 \times (-4)$$

(Firsts)   (Outsides)   (Insides)   (Lasts)

$$2k^2 \qquad -8k \qquad -3k \qquad 12$$

Two terms correct gains you the 1ˢᵗ mark

Q 1. *(a)*
$$3k + (2k - 3)(k - 4) \qquad \checkmark$$
$$= 3k + 2k^2 - 8k - 3k + 12 \qquad \checkmark$$
$$= 2k^2 - 8k + 12 \qquad \checkmark$$

3 marks

Complete brackets

- All 4 terms correct from multiplying out the brackets gains you this 2ⁿᵈ mark

Like terms

- You must 'tidy up' gathering all the like terms together and simplifying:

$$3k - 8k - 3k = -8k$$

See Int 2 Notes, Section 4, p. 12–14

Start to factorise

- $7m^2$ gives only one possibility namely $(7m \; ....)(m \; ....)$

- 16 has many possible factors:

$(....4)(....4)$ or $(....2)(....8)$ etc

Q1. *(b)*
$$7m^2 + 54m - 16 \qquad \checkmark$$
$$= (7m - 2)(m + 8) \qquad \checkmark$$

2 marks

Finish factoring

- When you think you have the correct combination then use "FOIL" to multiply the brackets out. If your answer is not $7m^2 + 54m - 16$ then try another combination!

See Int 2 Notes, Section 4, p. 16

Probability
- You have to identify those passengers who waited for more than 15 minutes. How many are there. Fortunately a stem-and-leaf diagram shows the numbers in increasing order.

  15 minutes would show up between the '2' and '8' in the 2nd row of the diagram. There are only 4 times greater than 15 namely:

  $$18, 21, 26 \text{ and } 30$$

- 4 passengers out of a total of 16 passengers gives a probability of $\frac{4}{16}$ or $\frac{1}{4}$.

  See Int 2 Notes, Section 9, p. 35–36

Q 2.

Probability $= \frac{4}{16} = \frac{1}{4}$ ✓

1 mark

Median (Q_2)
- Read the stem-and-leaf diagram left to right, top to bottom: this gives the data in increasing order:

  (85 93 101 102 107 109) 110 (113 114 117 119 119 120)

  The median is the middle value

Q 3. *(a)*(i)

Median = 110 minutes ✓

1 mark

Lower quartile (Q_1)
- This is the median of the lower 6 values i.e. The mean of the two middle values 101 and 102

Q3. *(a)*(ii)

Lower quartile $= \frac{101+102}{2} = 101\cdot5$ ✓

Upper quartile $= \frac{117+119}{2} = 118$

✓

2 marks

Upper quartile (Q_3)
- This is the median of the upper 6 values i.e. The mean of the two middle values 117 and 119

  See Int 2 Notes, Section 8, p. 31

End points
- You should first find the least and greatest values: in this case 85 and 120. This allows you to construct the scale

- Use the squared paper provided in your exam

Q 3.*(b)*

Boxplot of walk times

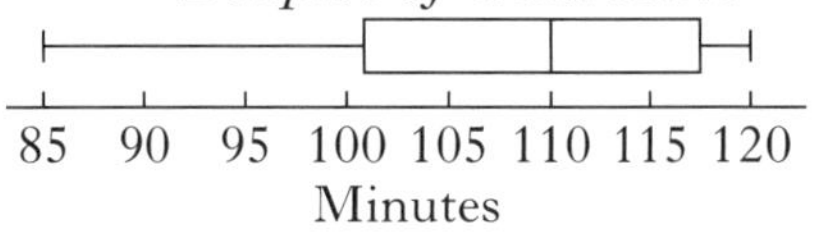

85 90 95 100 105 110 115 120 ✓
Minutes ✓

2 marks

Box
- Q_1 and Q_3 mark the ends of the box, in this case the values are $101\cdot5$ and 118

- Q_2 is shown by the line in the box, in this case the value is 110

  See Int 2 Notes, Section 8, p. 31

Q 4. *(a)*
gradient $= -\frac{1}{2}$ ✓

1 mark

Gradient
- Gradient $= \frac{\text{Distance up (or down)}}{\text{Distance along}}$. In this case the line goes 1 down, 2 along. 1 down is shown as -1 in the fraction: $\frac{-1}{2}$ giving $-\frac{1}{2}$

See Int 2 Notes, Section 3, p. 9

Q 4. *(b)*
Equation is: $y = -\frac{1}{2}x + 2$ ✓
✓
$(\Rightarrow 2y = -x + 4 \Rightarrow 2y + x = 4)$

2 marks

y-intercept
- The y-intercept is $(0, 2)$ giving $c = 2$

Equation
- You use '$y = mx + c$' with $m = -\frac{1}{2}$ and $c = 2$
- Further rearrangement is not essential

See Int 2 Notes, Section 3, p. 10–11

Q 4. *(c)*

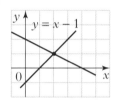

✓

The point of intersection is $(2,1)$ ✓

2 marks

2nd line
- $y = x - 1$ has gradient 1 (1 up, 1 along) and y-intercept $(0, -1)$

Intersection
- This can be read off the graph: the point where the two lines cross i.e. $(2,1)$
- Alternatively solve simultaneously:

$$\left. \begin{array}{l} y = -\frac{1}{2}x + 2 \\ y = x - 1 \end{array} \right\} \rightarrow \left. \begin{array}{l} 2y + x = 4 \\ y - x = -1 \end{array} \right\}$$

Add: $3y = 3 \Rightarrow y = 1$ etc

See Int 2 Notes, Section 3, p. 10

Q 5.
$\cos x° = 0.951$
$x°$ is in the 1ˢᵗ or 4ᵗʰ quadrants
The 1ˢᵗ quadrant angle is $18°$
The 4ᵗʰ quadrant angle is
$\qquad 360° - 18° = 342°$
So $x = 342$ is therefore another
$\qquad$ value ✓

1 mark

Value
- You have no calculator in paper 1. The information given in the question is the following: $\cos^{-1}(0.951) = 18°$ which is what you normally get from your calculator
- $\cos x°$ is positive. Use:

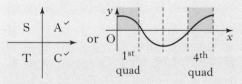

- The 4ᵗʰ quadrant angle is always given by:

$$360° - (1^{st}\text{ quadrant angle})$$

See Int 2 Notes, Section 12, p. 50

Q 6.

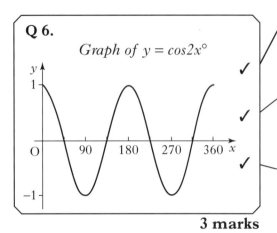

Graph of $y = \cos 2x°$

✓
✓
✓

3 marks

Amplitude
- The maximum value is 1 and the minimum value is −1. In general for the graph $y = k \cos ax$ the maximum value is k and the minimum value is $-k$ (for k positive). In this case $k = 1$.

Cycles
- There are 2 cycles from 0° to 360°. In general for $y = k \cos ax$ there will be 'a' cycles from 0° to 360°. In this case $a = 2$
- Take care to show clearly the scale you are using on each axis

Curve
- There is a mark given for the correct shape of graph. You should practice drawing the sine, cosine, and tangent graphs until you get good at drawing them correctly. You are not given these graphs in your exam – learn them!

See Int 2 Notes, Section 12, p. 48–49

Q 7.

$$a^{-3} \times (a^{-2})^{-2}$$
$$= a^{-3} \times a^{-2 \times (-2)}$$ ✓
$$= a^{-3} \times a^{4}$$
$$= a^{-3 + 4}$$
$$= a^{1} = a$$ ✓

2 marks

Power of a Power
- The Index Law used here is: $(a^m)^n = a^{mn}$
- Remember:
  negative × negative = positive

Multiplication
- The Index Law used here is: $a^m \times a^n = a^{m+n}$. Multiplying two numbers written as powers (with the same base) Then you add the indices.
- The index 1 in a^1 is not needed – just write a without any index.

See Int 2 Notes, Section 10, p. 41–42

Q 8. *(a)(i)*
The least value of $(2x − 3)^2 + 2$
is $0^2 + 2 = 2$ and this occurs when
$2x − 3 = 0$ ✓

$\Rightarrow 2x = 3 \Rightarrow x = \frac{3}{2}$ ✓

So P $\left(\frac{3}{2}, 2\right)$

2 marks

y-coordinate
- You will never get a negative value when you square a quantity so the minimum value of $(2x−3)^2$ is zero. This leads to the minimum value of $(2x−3)^2 + 2$ being 2.

x-coordinate
- The minimum value will occur when $(2x−3)^2$ is at its minimum of zero. This happens when you square zero so you require $2x − 3 = 0$

See Int 2 Notes, Section 11, p. 44

Q 8.(*a*)(ii)
For the y-intercept set $x = 0$
So $y = (2 \times 0 - 3)^2 + 2$
$= (-3)^2 + 2 = 9 + 2 = 11$
So Q(0,11)   ✓

1 mark

y-intercept
- All points on the y-axis have an x-coordinate of zero. This is why you set $x = 0$ in the equation of the parabola $y = (2x-3)^2 + 2$. Doing this gives you the y-intercept i.e $y = 11$

- You must write your answer in 'point format' i.e. (0,11) not just leave "$x = 0$ and $y = 11$"

Q 8.(*b*)

axis of symmetry

$y = 11$

Q   R

0      $\frac{3}{2}$ 3 x

✓

So R (3,11)   ✓

2 marks

Strategy
- All parabolas are symmetric. In this case the axis of symmetry passes through the minimum turning point $P\left(\frac{3}{2}, 2\right)$. The axis has equation $x = \frac{3}{2}$

- The axis of symmetry bisects QR as this diagram shows:

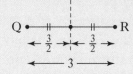

Coordinates
- R is on line $y = 11$ so its y-coordinate is 11

See Int 2 Notes, Section 11, p. 42

Q 9.(*a*)
Area = length × breadth
$= (x + 1)(x - 2)$ cm^2 ✓

1 mark

Area expression
- You are using the area of a rectangle formula here

Q 9.(*b*)

$\dfrac{\text{Frame}}{\text{Area}} = \begin{matrix}\text{Area of} \\ \text{outside} \\ \text{Rectangle}\end{matrix} - \begin{matrix}\text{Area of} \\ \text{Inside} \\ \text{Rectangle}\end{matrix}$ ✓

$= x(x + 3) - (x + 1)(x - 2)$
$= x^2 + 3x - (x^2 - 2x + x - 2)$
$= x^2 + 3x - x^2 + 2x - x + 2$
$= 4x + 2$ cm^2 ✓

2 marks

Strategy
- The frame is what is left when you remove the picture. This leads to the strategy of subtraction of the picture area (from part (a)) from the large rectangle area ($x \times (x + 3)$)

Simplification
- Brackets are essential in $(x^2 - 2x + x - 2)$ since you are subtracting all of this expression.

- The 'x^2' terms cancel and the like terms $3x$, $2x$ and $-x$ simplify to $4x$

See Int 2 Notes, Section 4, p. 12–14

WORKED ANSWERS: EXAM C ° **PAPER 2**

Q 1.
For x-intercept set $y = 0$
So $x^2 - 9 = 0$ ✓
$\Rightarrow x^2 = 9$
$\Rightarrow x = 3$ or -3
x-intercept are $(3, 0)$ and $(-3, 0)$ ✓

2 marks

Strategy
• All points on the x-axis have a y-coordinate of zero. This is why you substitute $y = 0$ in the equation of the graph to find where it intersects the x-axis.

Coordinates
• Solving $x^2 = 4$ there are two possibilities $x = 2$ (since $2^2 = 4$) and $x = -2$ (since $(-2^2 = 4)$).

Q 2.
A reduction of 22% means that 78% will be left giving a multiplication factor of 0·78 ✓
After 3 minutes:
N° of bacteria $= 250000 \times 0 \cdot 78^3$ ✓
$= 118638 \doteq 119000$
(to the nearest thousand) ✓

3 marks

Factor
• Notice: $78\% = \frac{78}{100} = 0 \cdot 78$

Strategy
• To find 78% of a quantity multiply by 0·78. Doing this 3 times $(0 \cdot 78 \times 0 \cdot 78 \times 0 \cdot 78)$ is equivalent to multiplying by $0 \cdot 78^3$

Calculation
• On your calculator $\times 0 \cdot 78^3$ is keyed as: $\boxed{\times}\boxed{0}\boxed{\cdot}\boxed{7}\boxed{8}\boxed{\wedge}\boxed{3}$. The key $\boxed{\wedge}$ means "raised to the power of".

• Any correct rounding is acceptable (or no rounding!)

See Int 2 Notes, Section 1, p. 5

Q 3.
Let size A weigh a kg and size B weigh b kg.
The 1ˢᵗ diagram gives:
$$3a + 2b = 94 \qquad ✓$$
The 2ⁿᵈ diagram gives:
$$2a + 3b = 101 \qquad ✓$$
Solve:

$$\left.\begin{array}{l} 3a + 2b = 94 \\ 2a + 3b = 101 \end{array}\right\} \begin{array}{l} \times 3 \rightarrow 9a + 6b = 282 \\ \times 2 \rightarrow 4a + 6b = 202 \end{array} ✓$$
$$\text{Subtract}: \quad \overline{5a \qquad = 80}$$

$$\Rightarrow a = \tfrac{80}{5} = 16$$
Substitute $a = 16$ in $3a + 2b = 94$
$$\Rightarrow 3 \times 16 + 2b = 94$$
$$\Rightarrow 48 + 2b = 94 \qquad ✓$$
$$\Rightarrow 2b = 94 - 48 = 46$$
$$\Rightarrow b = 23 \qquad ✓$$
One size A weight weighs 16 kg and one size B weight weighs 23 kg $\qquad ✓$

6 marks

Interpretation
- Make sure the two quantities you are to find are given letters and explain what the two letters are standing for

- Three Size A weights will weigh $3 \times a$ kg and two size B weights will weigh $2 \times b$ kg.

2ⁿᵈ equation
- Two Size A and three Size B weigh $2 \times a + 3 \times b$ kg

Strategy
- Two equations with two unknowns: you need to use 'simultaneous equations

Two values
- Following the method to produce two values will gain you this mark - even for the wrong values!

Correct values
- You should check the values work in the 'other' equation i.e. $2a + 3b = 101$

Statement
- Reread the question: what exactly did it ask you to find? Make sure you have done this!

See Int 2 Notes, Section 7, p. 25–27

Q 4. *(a)*

x	$x - \bar{x}$	$(x - \bar{x})^2$
503	2	4
504	3	9
497	−4	16
495	−6	36
506	5	25

$$\Sigma(x - \bar{x})^2 = 90$$

$$S = \sqrt{\frac{\Sigma\left(x - \bar{x}\right)^2}{n-1}} = \sqrt{\frac{90}{4}} \qquad ✓$$
$$= 4{\cdot}743\ldots \doteqdot 4{\cdot}7 \qquad ✓$$

(to 1 decimal place)

3 marks

Squared Deviations
- This mark is gained for correctly calculating the values in the last column of the table i.e $(x - \bar{x})^2$

- No negative values should ever appear in this column. Remember when you square a quantity your answer will be positive or zero

- The mean, $\bar{x}$, has been given to you in the question and so you do not need to calculate it again!

Substitution
- This mark is for correct substitution of the values $\Sigma(x - \bar{x})^2 = 90$ and $n - 1 = 4$ into the standard deviation formula

Calculation
- Remember always that there is a square root to be taken at the end of a standard deviation calculation

- Any reasonable rounding is acceptable

See Int 2 Notes, Section 9, p. 33–34

Q 4. *(b)*
Yes it did. The new standard deviation of 3·5 is less than the previous value of 4·7 so there was less variation about the mean. ✓

1 mark

Statement
- Your explanation must use the standard deviation statistics that you calculated in part(a) and are also given in the question. The greater the standard deviation the greater the variation about the mean (and vice versa).

Fraction
- The sector shown has a central angle of 40°. The complete circle has a central angle of 360°. Comparing 40° with 360° gives the fraction $\frac{40}{360}$
- Cancelling down is not essential but is neater.

Q 5.

Fraction of circle $= \frac{46}{360} = \frac{1}{9}$ ✓

So Shaded Area $= \frac{1}{9} \times \pi\, r^2$ ✓

where $r = \frac{2\cdot5}{2} = 1\cdot25$ metres

Shaded Area $= \frac{1}{9} \times \pi \times 1\cdot25^2$

$= 0\cdot5454....$

$\doteqdot 0\cdot545$ m^2 ✓

(correct to 3 significant figures)

3 marks

Strategy
- You have a sector that is $\frac{1}{9}$ of the complete circle and it will therefore have an area that is $\frac{1}{9}$ of πr^2. The diameter is given as 2·5 metres. Remember to half this before substitution into πr^2.

Calculation
- Always use the $\boxed{\pi}$ button on your calculator, not values like 3·14 unless the question asks you to do this
- Accuracy is not mentioned in the question so there is no mark awarded for rounding

See Int 2 Notes, Section 5, p. 17–18

Strategy
- Did you know to use the 'quadratic formula'? The clue is in the wording of the question: "correct to two decimal places". Accuracy is never mentioned in a quadratic equation question where you are expected to use 'factorisation'.

Q 6.

$11x^2 - 2x - 1 = 0$

compare $ax^2 + bx + c = 0$

$\Rightarrow a = 11$, $b = -2$ and $c = -1$

Now use $x = \frac{-b \pm \sqrt{b^2 - 4ac}}{2a}$ ✓

So $x = \frac{-(-2) \pm \sqrt{(-2)^2 - 4 \times 11 \times (-1)}}{2 \times 11}$ ✓

$x = \frac{2 \pm \sqrt{4 + 44}}{22}$

$\Rightarrow x = \frac{2 + \sqrt{48}}{22}$ or $x = \frac{2 - \sqrt{48}}{22}$ ✓

$\Rightarrow x = 0.4058...$ or $x = -0.2240...$

$\Rightarrow x \doteqdot 0.41$ or $x \doteqdot -0.22$ ✓

(both roots correct to 2 decimal places)

4 marks

Substitution
- The values for a, b and c must also include the negative sign if it is there. In this case both b and c are negative. Take care over this.

b²–4ac
- The discriminant is the number under the square root sign. It is the hardest part to calculate when using this formula. Carefully keying in the whole calculation $(-2)^2 - 4 \times 11 \times (-1)$ should work but be aware:

  $\boxed{-}\boxed{2}\boxed{x^2}$ and $\boxed{(}\boxed{-}\boxed{2}\boxed{)}\boxed{x^2}$ give different answers. In this case the brackets are essential!

Calculation
- First find the answer to $2 + \sqrt{48}$ (or $2 - \sqrt{48}$) and only then divide by 22
- Accuracy is important so round as instructed.

See Int 2 Notes, Section 11, p. 45–46

Q 7. *(a)*

Extend line AB (see diagram)

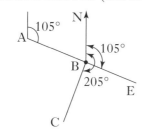

$\angle NBE = 105°$

So $\angle CBE = 205° - 105°$

$= 100°$

So $\angle ABC = 180° - 100°$

$= 80°$ ✓

(since $A\hat{B}E$ is a straight angle)

1 mark

Angle
- It is essential to bring the 105° information at vertex A to vertex B. This can be done by extending the line AB
- An alternative is:

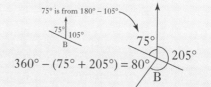

$360° - (75° + 205°) = 80°$

Q 7. *(b)*

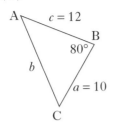

Use the Cosine Rule in triangle ABC: ✓

$b^2 = a^2 + c^2 - 2ac \cos B$

$\quad = 10^2 + 12^2 - 2 \times 10 \times 12 \times \cos 80°$

$\quad = 202 \cdot 32....$ ✓

$\qquad$ So $b = \sqrt{202 \cdot 32....}$

$\qquad\qquad = 14 \cdot 22... \doteq 14 \cdot 2$ km ✓

The required distance is 14·2 km (to 1 dec pl)

3 marks

Strategy
- Two sides and the included angle all known means the Cosine Rule should be used

Substitution
- The version given on your formulae page is:

$$a^2 = b^2 + c^2 - 2bc \cos A$$

You must be able to change this to find side b:

$$b^2 = a^2 + c^2 - 2ac \cos B$$

Practice this!

Calculation
- Remember the square root at the end.

See Int 2 Notes, Section 6, p. 24

Q 7. *(c)*

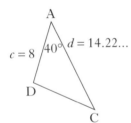

Area of triangle ADC

$= \frac{1}{2} cd \sin A$ ✓

$= \frac{1}{2} \times 8 \times 14 \cdot 22... \times \sin 40°$

$= 36 \cdot 57....$

$\doteq 36 \cdot 6$

Required area is 36·6 km² ✓
(correct to 1 decimal place)

2 marks

Strategy
- This is not a right-angled triangle so the 'trig' area formula will have to be used. The formula given in your exam is:

Area $= \frac{1}{2} ab \sin C$

You should adapt this for triangle ACD:

Area $= \frac{1}{2} cd \sin A$

- The formula always involves two sides and the angle in between them (the included angle).

Calculation
- Do not use rounded answers in subsequent calculations. In this case using the rounded answer 14·2 km from part *(b)* gives an answer of 36·5 km². You cannot say this is accurate to 1 decimal place!

See Int 2 Notes, Section 6, p. 22

Substitution

- This 1st mark is for correctly substituting the values $r = 2$ cm and $h = 6$ cm into the Cone formula

- The formula is given to you on your formulae page during your exam

- The radius (r) is used in the formula. You are given the diameter (4 cm) and so need to halve this

Q 8. *(a)*

Volume of cone $= \frac{1}{3}\pi r^2 h$

with $r = \frac{4}{2} = 2$ cm and $h = 6$ cm

So Volume $= \frac{1}{3} \times \pi 2^2 \times 6$ ✓

$\qquad = 25 \cdot 132....$ ✓

$\qquad \doteqdot 25 \cdot 1$ cm^3

$\qquad$ (to 1 dec pl.) ✓

3 marks

Calculation

- Remember to use the $\boxed{\pi}$ button (not $3 \cdot 14$)

Rounding

- There is a mark allocated for correct rounding to 3 significant figures. An answer of 25 cm^3 would not gain this mark – it's only got 2 sig figs!

See Int 2 Notes, Section 2, p. 8

Volume of weight

- Correct substitution in $\frac{1}{2}\pi r^2 h$ gains this mark

Equation

- Setting the volume of the weight equal to the volume of the cone calculated in part (a) is the strategy for finding h.

- Don't use $25 \cdot 1$ cm^3 – This was rounded.

Q 8. *(b)*

Volume of a cylinder $= \pi r^2 h$

So Volume of the weight

$\qquad = \frac{1}{2}\pi r^2 h$

where $r = 2$ cm, Volume

$\qquad = 25 \cdot 132...$ cm^3 and h is

$\qquad$ not known

$\Rightarrow 25 \cdot 132... = \frac{1}{2} \times \pi \times 2^2 \times h$ ✓

$\Rightarrow 25 \cdot 132... = 2\pi \times h$ ✓

$\Rightarrow h = \frac{25 \cdot 132....}{2\pi} = 4$ ✓

The height of the weight is 4 cm

3 marks

Solving

- Solve the equation to gain this mark

- You might wonder at exactly 4 cm being the solution. Is it exactly 4? Yes it is:

$\frac{1}{3}\pi \times 2^2 \times 6 = \frac{1}{2}\pi \times 2^2 \times h$

$\qquad$ (divide by $\pi \times 2^2$)

$\Rightarrow \frac{1}{3} \times 6 = \frac{1}{2}h \Rightarrow 2 = \frac{1}{2}h \Rightarrow h = 4$

This proof uses the 'exact' expression for the volume of the cone from part (a).

See Int 2 Notes, Section 2, p. 8

Value of tan$x°$
- The 1st step is to find the value of tan$x°$ i.e. solve the equation for 'tan$x°$'

1st value
- tan$x°$ will be positive if $x°$ is in the 1st or 3rd quadrants. Use:

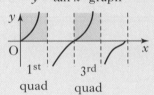

(Quadrant diagram)

or

$y = \tan x°$ graph

- The angle is calculated using $\tan^{-1}\left(\frac{15}{2}\right)$

Q 9. *(a)*
$2\tan x° - 15 = 0$
$\Rightarrow 2\tan x° = 15$
$\Rightarrow \tan x° = \frac{15}{2}$ ✓
$x°$ is in the 1st or 3rd quadrants ✓
1st quadrant angle is $82\cdot4°$ ✓
so $x = 82\cdot4$ or $x = 180 + 82\cdot4$
$= 262\cdot4$ ✓
(correct to 1 decimal place)

3 marks

2nd value
- 3rd quadrant angle is always given by:
$180° + (1\text{st quadrant angle})$
See Int 2 Notes, Section 12, p. 50

Strategy
- replace tan$x°$ with $\frac{\sin x°}{\cos x°}$
- The formula $\tan x° = \frac{\sin x°}{\cos x°}$ is not given to you in the exam. Learn it!

Q 9. *(b)*
$$\frac{\sin x°}{\tan x°} = \frac{\sin x°}{\sin x°/\cos x°}$$ ✓
$$= \frac{\sin x° \times \cos x°}{\sin x°/\cos x° \times \cos x°} = \frac{\sin x° \cos x°}{\sin x°}$$
$$= \cos x°$$ ✓

2 marks

Simplify
- Multiply 'top' and 'bottom' by cos$x°$. The two cos$x°$ terms cancel. Then the two sin$x°$ terms cancel
- Choose any angle, say 17°, and check on your calculator. Does cos17° give the same as $\frac{\sin 17°}{\tan 17°}$?
See Int 2 Notes, Section 12, p. 51

Q 10. *(a)*
$$\angle AOB = \left(\frac{360}{5}\right)° = 72°$$ ✓

1 mark

Angle
- There would be 5 equal angles around O if the other radii were drawn in. So each angle is $\frac{1}{5}$ of 360°.

Q 10. *(b)*

Draw ON, the altitude of triangle AOB

ON bisects angle AOB so Angle AON = 36° ✓

In triangle AON, $\sin 36° = \frac{AN}{5}$ ✓

$\Rightarrow AN = 5 \sin 36° = 2 \cdot 938...$

So $AB = 2 \times AN = 2 \times 2 \cdot 938...$
$= 5 \cdot 877...$

So $AB \doteqdot 5 \cdot 88$ cm ✓
(to 3 significant figures)

3 marks

Strategy

• Create a right-angled triangle and use 'SOHCAHTOA'

• Alternatively you could use the Sine Rule in triangle AOB (The angles are 72°, 54° and 54°)

SOHCAHTOA

• In triangle OAN you are trying to find the 'Opposite' and you know the 'Hypotenuse' This gives SOHCAHTOA so use 'sin'

Side length

• By the symmetry of the diagram, doubling your answer for the length AN will give the length AB

See Int 2 Notes, Section 5, p. 20
Section 6, p. 21

Q 11. *(a)*

$$\frac{5}{\sqrt{3}} = \frac{5 \times \sqrt{3}}{\sqrt{3} \times \sqrt{3}}$$ ✓

$$= \frac{5\sqrt{3}}{3}$$ ✓

2 marks

Rationalise

• The number $\sqrt{3}$ in the denominator is not a rational number, it is a surd

• Multiplying 'top' and 'bottom' by $\sqrt{3}$ gives a rational denominator of 3

Simplify

• $5 \times \sqrt{3}$ is written as $5\sqrt{3}$ and $\sqrt{3} \times \sqrt{3}$ is written as 3

• No further simplification is possible. Don't be tempted to cancel the '3's. Since the 'top' 3 is under a square root sign it is not available for cancelling

See Int 2 Notes, Section 10, p. 41

Q 11. *(b)*

$$\frac{2}{a} - \frac{1}{b}$$

$$= \frac{2b}{ab} - \frac{a}{ab} = \frac{2b-a}{ab}$$ ✓ ✓

2 marks

Common Denominator
- Consider a numerical example:

$\frac{2}{3} - \frac{1}{4}$ You cannot subtract quarters from thirds. The denominators are changed both to 12 by multiplying each fraction, 'top' and 'bottom' by a suitable number:

$\frac{2\times4}{3\times4} - \frac{1\times3}{4\times3} = \frac{8}{12} - \frac{3}{12}$. These can now be subtracted to give $\frac{8-3}{12} = \frac{5}{12}$.

Similarly $\frac{2}{a} - \frac{1}{b}$ cannot be subtracted unless the denominators are made equal:

$\frac{2\times b}{a\times b} - \frac{1\times a}{b\times a} = \frac{2b}{ab} - \frac{a}{ab}$

Simplify
- The final step is to subtract the numerators

See Int 2 Notes, Section 10, p. 38–39

Q 11. *(c)*

$$\frac{A}{p-q} = r$$

$$\Rightarrow A = r\,(p - q)$$ ✓

$$\Rightarrow \frac{A}{r} = p - q$$ ✓

$$\Rightarrow \frac{A}{r} + q = p$$

$$\text{So } p = \frac{A}{r} + q$$ ✓

3 marks

1st step
- Multiply both sides of the equation by $(p - q)$
- Brackets are needed: $r(p - q)$ is different from $rp - q$

2nd step
- Divide both sides of the equation by r

3rd step
- Add q to both sides of the equation
- Alternatively: $A = rp - rq \Rightarrow A + rq = rp$

$$\Rightarrow \frac{A+rq}{r} = p \text{ So } p = \frac{A+rq}{r}$$

See Int 2 Notes, Section 10, p. 38–39